Edward Brown

Poultry Fattening

A practical guide to the fattening, killing, shaping, dressing, and marketing of chickens, ducks, geese, and turkeys

Edward Brown

Poultry Fattening

A practical guide to the fattening, killing, shaping, dressing, and marketing of chickens, ducks, geese, and turkeys

ISBN/EAN: 9783337292157

Printed in Europe, USA, Canada, Australia, Japan

Cover: Foto ©Lupo / pixelio.de

More available books at **www.hansebooks.com**

POULTRY FATTENING

A PRACTICAL GUIDE TO THE FATTENING, KILLING, SHAPING, DRESSING, AND MARKETING OF CHICKENS, DUCKS, GEESE, AND TURKEYS

BY

EDWARD BROWN, F.L.S.

Lecturer on Aviculture at the Reading College, to the Essex, Cumberland, Hampshire, Kent, Lincolnshire, Northumberland, Worcestershire, Yorkshire, and other County Councils; Author of "Poultry Keeping as an Industry for Farmers and Cottagers," "Industrial Poultry Keeping," "Pleasurable Poultry Keeping," &c.; Judge of Table Poultry at the Royal Agricultural Society's Shows, &c.

WITH ILLUSTRATIONS

EDWARD ARNOLD

LONDON	NEW YORK
37, BEDFORD STREET	70, FIFTH AVENUE

SIR WALTER GILBEY, BART.,

PRESIDENT

OF THE

ROYAL AGRICULTURAL SOCIETY

OF

ENGLAND

1895–6.

CONTENTS.

		PAGE
INTRODUCTION	. . . .	13

CHAP.		
I.	BREEDS AND CROSSES . .	29
II.	HATCHING AND REARING . .	41
III.	SHEDS AND PENS . . .	51
IV.	POULTRY FATTENING IN ENGLAND	63
V.	FATTENING FOWLS IN FRANCE	73
VI.	KILLING AND SHAPING .	85
VII.	"PETITS POUSSINS" AND BROILERS .	98
VIII.	FATTENING DUCKS . . .	108
IX.	FATTENING GEESE	120
X.	FATTENING TURKEYS AND GUINEA-FOWLS	128
XI.	MARKETING TABLE POULTRY . . .	136
XII.	TABLE POULTRY EXHIBITIONS . .	147

LIST OF ILLUSTRATIONS.

INTERIOR OF FATTENING SHED, IVILLE FARM, BAYNARDS . . . . . *Frontispiece*

FIG.		PAGE
1.	ANCIENT EGYPTIAN CRAMMING GEESE	13
2.	OUTSIDE FATTENING PENS AT BUXTED, SUSSEX	46
3.	AMERICAN REARING-HOUSE	49
4.	FATTENING SHED AT BUXTED, SUSSEX	53
5.	CALWAY'S FATTENING PEN	54
6.	PENS IN HEATHFIELD FATTENING SHED	56
7.	FRONT VIEW, BAYNARDS PENS	57
8.	FATTENING AND KILLING SHEDS, GAMBAIS, FRANCE	58
9.	SUSSEX COLLECTOR WITH CAGE ON BACK	65
10.	"HEARSON" CRAMMER	67
11.	FUNNEL FOR FATTENING	81
12.	ODILE-MARTIN FATTENING CAGE	82
13.	SHAPING-TROUGH	88
14.	SHAPED SUSSEX FOWL (*breast downwards*)	89
15.	,, ,, ,, (*breast upwards*)	90
16.	FRENCH SHAPING-BOARD	92
17.	SHAPING-CLOTH FOR ABOVE BOARD	92
18.	LA FLÈCHE DEAD POULTRY	93
19.	LA BRESSE SHAPING-CLOTH	94
20.	LA BRESSE DEAD POULTRY	96

PREFACE.

By Mr. Charles Edward Brooke,

Past-Master of the Worshipful Poulters' Company of London.

As a Past-Master of the Poulters' Company of London, I very willingly accepted the proffered opportunity of glancing through the following pages, while they were still in manuscript form, and it appears to me, albeit a work necessarily dealing with theory as much as with experience, to be an exceedingly useful and suggestive treatise on the pre-eminently practical question of fattening table poultry for the market.

I am now asked to give my own views, and with that request I readily comply, in the hope that these remarks may be accepted as a friendly send-off to a book which I regard as a welcome addition to our literature on this subject. The author, divesting himself as far as may be of mere theory, has diligently, and in a thorough-going spirit, set himself the task of solving many difficult problems which have often puzzled the less initiated. He has very properly insisted on the canons to be observed, both in the selection of stock and in the methodical care to be bestowed on poultry, and thus points out the easiest way to a pleasurable occupation, open to the humblest of our artisans and cottagers, and above all to an industry which, in view of our large annual imports in this particular department, may be developed to an almost unlimited extent. Nor is there, as he clearly shows, any valid reason why we should not produce table poultry under conditions as favourable as those which prevail elsewhere, especially in France.

It is a satisfaction to all who are labouring to promote poultry breeding, on a rational and lucrative basis, to know that our authorities are moving in the right direction.

I may cite the many gratifying examples of success brought to the notice of Mr. R. Henry Rew, who, in pursuance of a decision of the Royal Commission on Agriculture, has been inquiring into the actual state of the poultry rearing and fattening industry of the Heathfield district of Sussex.

One of these cases, a fairly typical one, shows how a start may be made. The man referred to was employed as a farm labourer, receiving 15s. per week wages, out of which he paid 2s. per week for his cottage, to which a good garden was attached. His employer lent him 24 hens and 2 male birds, with a movable house, and allowed him to run the fowls over his fields. From this stock he reared chickens all the year round, selling them at prices ranging from 1s. 8d. to 3s. 6d. each, and contriving by good management to secure a large number in April, when they brought him most profit. He spent £17 in food, but at the end of the twelve months had realised a clear gain of £20, and after returning the 26 stock fowls had still some left with which to resume operations. No doubt from this he will go on, and, with ordinary good fortune, soon be on the road towards becoming a small holder.

In another case, that of a 200 acre farm, where both rearing and fattening are conducted on a large scale, the detailed accounts of sales of poultry for a whole year exhibit equally encouraging results, viz., after paying interest at 5 per cent. on £600 capital, there remained a substantial profit of £268. The prices obtained by rearers range from 1s. 8d. in summer to 3s. 6d., or even 4s., each fowl, the highest point reached being in May. After June this scale recedes at a rapid rate. A prosperous farmer, whose chickens were sold to a Heathfield higgler at 3s. 6d. each in April, made the apparently astonishing statement to Mr. Rew, that if 100 hens are properly looked after they will yield a larger return in twelve months than 100 breeding ewes.

What should prove most encouraging to small cottagers in the rearing of chickens for the market, is, that fowls are almost omnivorous; not only do they eat grain and vegetables, but they absolutely require variety of food, including meat or fat, and so scraps from the household may always be mixed with daily rations, and thus all leavings are utilised. In some instances numbers of coops, representing as many broods of chickens, are set out under the hedges in public highways, and it is not surprising that the chickens reared under these circumstances should thrive often better than elsewhere. The grit from the roads, and the insect life in the hedges, conduce to their general health.

One of the most discouraging features of chicken rearing by those who have not mastered the first principles of the industry is that distempers sometimes break out, from a lack of absolute cleanliness about the pens, or from the absence of a regular supply of grit or ground oyster-shells, and the very indispensable dust bath. Hence the infection of poultry on adjacent premises. Frequent lime-washing is a great preventive of disease. Weakness resulting from want of variety in feeding may be cured by a meat diet. I have been told that bullock's heart is a sovereign panacea for several of the ills that occasionally affect the chicken yard. Above all, the beginner must be cautioned against strewing the ground with vegetable leaves or remnants, which should be kept from under the fowls' feet by being cut up and placed in troughs. Experience has invariably shown that the dragging about of any kind of food in filth is one of the chief causes of disease. Some consider that a good plan is to place meat and vegetables on clean sacks laid on the ground, and covered with panels of wire netting $1\frac{1}{2}$ inches in the mesh, through which the birds can pick up what they need. Russian white oats are strongly recommended as not only best for poultry, but as being cheaper than our own produce.

With regard to the fattening process, which is carried on in a special building, well shaded from the light, I have always recommended the use of barred coops (one for each bird), although in Sussex generally several birds are put together. These may be placed in horizontal tiers one above the other, the bottom of the cage, over the tray, consisting of flat bars rounded at the edges, 2 inches in width at the top, and tapering away beneath, so that the droppings may fall freely into the receptacle below the bars. Here the birds are confined for twenty-one days, the process being begun when they are three months old in summer, and four in winter. For the first week the food should consist of ground oats mixed with milk, in a moderately liquid state; mutton fat chopped fine and boiled with the milk is an excellent ingredient with the ground oats or buckwheat. During the last fortnight the fowls are crammed, either by machine or hand, with a mixture of barley-meal, oatmeal, and skim milk, together with beef and mutton fat, which is proportionately increased from day to day. The hard trimmings of loins of mutton are first boiled, and the liquid part poured on to the meal, with the scalding water, some coarse sand or gravel being added in order to facilitate digestion. Chickens fed in this manner twice a day, for a period of three weeks or a little longer, are then ready for the market.

To ensure a really presentable appearance, from the salesman's point of view, they should be fasted, *i.e.*, kept without food or water eighteen hours before killing, plucked while still warm, and this without "barking" the skin, and then be tied loosely at the hocks, pressed in the shaping board for four or five hours, packed in baskets or hampers, with some straw or paper between each layer. They may finally be delivered to the carriers, whose charge in the Heathfield district, and around Uckfield, for collecting and delivering to market, including the freightage by rail, is only 1s. per dozen.

If I have been thus explicit on these various points of detail, it is with the object of impressing upon the less experienced poultry breeder the importance of overcoming some constantly recurring obstacles to sound success. I consider Mr. Brown's work valuable as a guide to every-day practice, and invaluable as a book of reference. It certainly ought to be in the hands of all who desire to improve a neglected industry, and should be included in every parish library, so as to be within easy reach of those who are certain to benefit by its teaching.

45, FINSBURY SQUARE, E.C.
July, 1895.

INTRODUCTION.

For a long period of time, among the dainties or finer dishes for the table, fowls of various kinds have been recognised as holding a leading place. Even as far back as the days of Solomon we find in Scripture

Fig. 1.—Ancient Egyptian Cramming Geese.

references to "fatted fowls," though whether these words apply to ordinary poultry is a point which has led to some discussion. We may, however, leave this controversial subject on one side, for there can be no question that 4,000 years ago the ancient Egyptians crammed their geese, and probably were the originators of the cramming system, as they appear to have been in respect to artificial incubation. The drawing given on page 13 (Fig. 1), copied from one of the tablets in the Pyramid of Sakkara, represents a man engaged in the work of cramming geese by means of patons, or boluses, of food, practically identical with the system adopted in some parts of France to-day. References could be given innumerable proving that this system is by no means new, but we need not dwell on them at any length. It is enough to show that the principle involved is recognised in nearly all branches of animal and plant life, utilised as food for man, and it is, as a matter of fact, as sensible to kill lean poultry as it would be to slaughter lean cattle or sheep. Even those who state their preference for taking a bird out of the farmyard, killing and eating it without any preparation, believe in feeding off cattle, sheep, and pigs, and would never think of selling to the butcher these animals in store condition. We simply ask them, therefore, to apply the same principles to poultry as to larger stock. It will be our object in this work to explain as fully as possible the methods adopted both at home and abroad, in the hope that the knowledge thus imparted may lead to an extension of the system.

At the outset it will be well to inquire what are the direct results of fattening fowls, and, as the matter must necessarily be one of £ s. d., how far success can be measured between those who fatten and those who do not adopt this system. Taking the London ard

Paris markets, which are but examples of others, we find that those fowls which command the best prices and are in the greatest demand, have been fatted or fed up. It may be well, however, to discount objections by stating that the term "fatted" is not a good word to describe the system. We do not mean that the fowls should be covered with a large quantity of oily fat, but really that the flesh carried upon the body shall be increased in quantity, and softened, or, to use a better term, ripened.

The difference between a well-fed table fowl and one which has not been subjected to this process is evident, and especially to those who have inquired into the system. If we take the prices realised by fowls, we find that those coming from districts where the fattening system is in vogue, are much higher than when sent in a lean condition, and in accordance with the completeness of the process so are the results attained. For instance, in the spring of the year the wholesale value of fowls of the ordinary type will range from 2s. 6d. to 4s. 6d. each, whereas well fed Surrey birds will bring from 5s. 6d. to 7s., and even more, per specimen. There can be no doubt that there is an abundance of room for the best qualities. Competition is greatest in every branch of industry amongst the ordinary classes, while those which are first-rate in quality will readily sell, and at greatly enhanced prices. Many figures could be given as to returns obtained in this way both at home and abroad, and it is not too much to say that those who produce the best can almost always find a market for· their produce at remunerative prices.

Until a recent period the process of fattening fowls has been almost entirely confined to the counties of Surrey, Sussex, and a part of Kent, in England, with a result that the table poultry trade has largely, so far as the best qualities are concerned, passed into the hands of those counties, which supply the finest specimens for our home market. I am not without hope that other districts will take up the industry, and recently was consulted by a gentleman who has started a fattening establishment in Scotland—the first, we believe, in that country. It may be of interest to record here a fact which is very suggestive. The gentleman referred to came to see me, and I strongly urged him before commencing operations to interview the people who would be his best customers, namely, poulterers in Edinburgh and Glasgow. He did so, and one leading poulterer in the Clydeside city named, when told what he proposed to do, asked a very pertinent question, " What class of fowls do you intend to send? If you are going to market third and fourth-rate stuff, such as we obtain from Ireland, we can get as much of that as we want. But, if you will let us have really first-rate fatted birds, such as we have now to obtain from London, we can take 500 a week during the season, and at good prices." This was encouragement enough, and is typical of what could be found in other parts of the country.

Some time ago I undertook an exhaustive inquiry over the whole of Great Britain as to the supplies of poultry. As a result it was found that London is the great centre of the trade, at any rate for the higher class qualities, though Liverpool supplies a large quantity of good Irish poultry, principally from the Wexford district, where fattening is carried on to some extent, and might be enormously developed. The result of this inquiry may be summarised as showing that in order to obtain a regular supply traders are compelled to depend chiefly upon the London market. These observations extended from Aberdeen to Plymouth. For instance, one dealer at Bournemouth told me that he buys all his poultry without exception from London, having tried several times to obtain local supplies, but the result was never satisfactory, as they were poor and irregular, and he has been compelled to look entirely to the metropolis. Now he can order all he requires by the evening's post, and they are delivered in abundance of time for dinner the following day. Local supplies are not only inferior in quality, but cannot be relied upon, and that would be destructive to his trade. In Leamington a similar statement was made, and in Manchester, which is one of our best provincial markets, whilst they have good birds from Ireland, and obtain the greater part of their supplies from that country, still most of their best chickens have until recently come from London. A further example will suffice as evidence of what is stated here, namely, that when in Aberdeen some time ago, I learnt that one of the leading hotels there used 100 chickens per week, all of which were obtained from London. This may be exceptional, but it is undoubtedly a case which shows that, although the north-east of Scotland produces some of the best Dorkings we have in the country, yet so irregular is the supply and so uncertain the quality, they find it pays them to bring their birds a distance of 520 miles.

It might naturally be assumed from these facts that there are special conditions giving the south-eastern district of England an advantage over other parts of the country. It would be folly to question that undoubtedly the counties of Surrey, Sussex, and Kent are well suited to this work, but they have no exceptional advantages over other districts which can be named. Probably the origin of the concentration there is explainable by the class of fowl kept, and by contiguity to the metropolis, which at one period, ere the railway era, was a very important matter, but in these days when distance is to a great extent annihilated, the special advantages do not apply. For a very long time—longer in fact than we can recall—the best class of poultry for table purposes has been bred more especially in Sussex and West Kent, and thus we see an explanation as to the development of this industry. Or, as stated in Mr. R. H. Rew's report, to be again noted : " It was suggested to me that the existence of a native kind of fowls of superior excellence for the table, and having an accommodating propensity to sit early and often, led the inhabitants, on recognising their good qualities, to devote special attention to the rearing and fattening of them. I am bound to say that, apart from actual evidence, it seems quite as probable that the industry developed the fowls as that the fowls originated the industry. In other words, the undoubted adaptability of the fowls to its particular ends may be the effect and not the cause of the attention given to their rearing and breeding."

Every one who has studied the development of various pursuits knows how great is the tendency towards concentration, and when combined with an absolute neglect of poultry keeping elsewhere, with a feeling that it is an unprofitable pursuit, far beneath the notice of agriculturists, the trade naturally passed into a comparatively limited area. But when we look at the matter a little more closely, what do we find? That Dorkings can be bred as successfully in the north of Scotland, in the north of Ireland, in Cumberland and Westmoreland, as in Surrey. Given that fact, the question of fattening is by no means difficult. We can by proper buildings and other arrangements overcome any atmospheric influences there may be so long as the birds themselves are produced. If Aberdeen can produce some of the best beef that is to be found anywhere, it is equally suitable for the production of table poultry, and thus the question of latitude is by no means as important as many people imagine.

Referring again to the Surrey, Kent, and Sussex districts, the well-known firm of Messrs. Brooke Bros., of Smithfield Market, London, have given me the following figures, the total amount paid by them to senders in the counties of Surrey, Kent, and Sussex alone in 1891-2 :—

	£	s.	d.
July, 1891	2,270	0	0
August	1,770	0	0
September	1,180	0	0
October	2,000	0	0
November	1,740	0	0
December	1,300	0	0
January, 1892	950	0	0

	£	s.	d.
February	800	0	0
March	850	0	0
April	1,050	0	0
May	1,240	0	0
June	1,750	0	0
	£16,900	0	0

In giving these figures, which do not include the large quantities they receive from other parts of England, from Ireland, and the Continent, Messrs. Brooke Bros. say: "We are of opinion that this may be taken to represent one-eighth of the total supply coming to London (from the counties named), and the average value of the fowls may be reckoned at a little under 3s. 4d. each net." On the basis given this firm sold upwards of 100,000 fowls from the three counties given above.

The same firm has furnished me with the average value of Sussex poultry sold by them during one complete year:—

	s.	d.		s.	d.
January	3	6			
February	3	6			
March	3	9			
April	4	6	to	5	0
May	4	3	„	4	9
June	3	9			
July	2	9			
August	2	6			
September	2	9			
October	2	6			
November	2	9			
December	3	0			

These figures show that the average for the first six

months was 4s. 1d. per head; for the second six months 2s. 8d. per head; and for the entire year just over 3s. 4d. per head. The above figures, however, represent all qualities, and it may be well to quote returns given by Mr. Rew, as to the prices obtained by "a large rearer and fattener who aims at maintaining a high reputation for his chickens, and who, therefore, probably secured rather more than the average prices at market":—

	s. d.	s. d.	
January	3 0	to 5 0	
February	3 0	„ 5 0	
March	4 0	„ 5 6	
April	5 0	„ 6 0	
May	5 0	„ 6 6	(10 sold at 7s.)
June	4 0	„ 6 0	
July	4 0	„ 5 6	
August	2 6	„ 4 0	
September	3 0	„ 3 9	
October	3 0	„ 3 6	
November	3 0	„ 3 6	
December	3 0	„ 4 9	

It will be seen that the averages here represented are considerably in excess of those given by the Messrs. Brooke Bros., and may be taken as representing the best qualities. If we take the mean value, it is to find that the average for the first six months was 4s. 10d. per head; for the second six months 3s. 7½d. per head; and for the entire year nearly 4s. 3d. per head.

This, of course, only represents a portion of the trade, and I may be permitted to quote from some figures which were given by me in the "Live Stock Journal Almanack" for 1894, showing what is done in one district, but which I have modified a little in accordance with later information.

By the courtesy of the London, Brighton and South Coast Railway, I am able to give the figures showing the extent of traffic in dead poultry from Heathfield. The following figures are for six months, representing about half the year's trade:—

	By Goods Train.		By Passenger Train.		Total.	
	tons	cwt.	tons	cwt.	tons	cwt.
September, 1892	141	19	18	11	160	10
October	133	1	16	12	149	13
November	121	2	13	2	134	4
January, 1893	72	4	11	0	83	4
February	64	6	8	8	72	14
March	66	9	10	5	76	14
	599	1	77	18	676	19

The year's operations consist of six busy and six slack months, and the above table gives the returns for three of each. From this it will be seen that from April, 1892, to March, 1893, the railway company conveyed certainly not less than 1,350 tons of dead poultry from this one station. If the average weight of each bird were four pounds, and probably, taking one season with another, this would be fair, for the largest birds are not produced at Heathfield, that represents more than three-quarters of a million fowls (750,000), truly a marvellous result. What the total extent of the Sussex trade in poultry is we have not been able definitely to obtain, but, inclusive of other districts, it probably exceeds 2,000 tons per annum, which on the same ratio means 1,112,000 fowls. The exact value of the trade is not easily determined, for the variation in value, both by reason of size and season, is great. But the salesmen referred to already inform me that their average for twelve months was 3s. 4d. Allowing the odd fourpence for carriage, commission, and expenses (which is above the actual cost), at 3s. each, this would give us the total of £112,500 for Heathfield, or for the entire county, if our approximation be correct, £166,800. And I am certain those who know will realise that I am not overstating the case, but rather the reverse. In the Uckfield district the chief villages at which cramming takes place are Hurstwood, Hadlow Down, Buxted, Framfield, Barnett Wood, Eason Green, and Black Boys, and Messrs. Bourner & Co., of Uckfield, who are the carriers thence, inform me that in 1894 they took from these villages, for the rail, 313 tons 16 cwt. 2 qr. 13 lb. of chickens, or 117,163 birds.

There is another most important fact which must be stated here, namely, that the commencement of fattening establishments in different parts of the country would have a most beneficial influence upon ordinary poultry keepers, creating a great demand for young birds. It is no uncommon thing in the Heathfield district for the higglers to pay up to 3s. 6d. for early hatched, well-grown chickens, of eight or ten weeks old, and so enormous is the demand for birds during the spring of the year, that something like 300,000 Irish chickens are brought over annually, at a cost of about $4\frac{1}{2}$d. each for carriage, to be fatted and sent out. The complaint in many parts of the country is that chickens cannot be sold at remunerative prices, and so long as no effort is put forth to properly prepare them for market this state of things will continue. I see no reason why almost every county in Britain should not have fattening establishments, thus supplying its own needs.

Reference has been made to Mr. R. Henry Rew's report to the Royal Commission on Agriculture,* by which official impress is given to facts only known to a few before, and it is to be hoped that this valuable report will be widely read and studied. Several instances are given as to the economic results of poultry rearing and fattening which are most suggestive, but one of these will suffice :—

" One of the most noteworthy instances which came under my notice was that of a young man whose farm of twenty-seven acres I visited. He had just purchased the holding and had been in possession about six months. He was thirty-three years of age and started life as a labourer. He struck me as being unusually intelligent, thrifty, and hard-working—in fact he attributed his success entirely to unremitting work. Every day, he said, week in and week out, he worked as long as there was daylight. But he formed a striking example of what can be done by means of poultry, for he began with rearing a few fowls, gradually increased his stock, and then started fattening, and so step by step, attained his present independent position. He had at the time of my visit a large

* Report by Mr. R. Henry Rew (Assistant Commissioner) on the " Poultry Rearing and Fattening Industry of the Heathfield District of Sussex." London : Eyre and Spottiswoode, 1894. Price 3d.

number of coops in a nine-acre field of grass, which had been laid down three years previously. He rears about 600 chickens himself, and collects once a week for his fattening shed, being away the whole day with his horse and cart. He showed me his horse, of which he was evidently and justifiably proud—a handsome mare which might very probably be worth £40. He had five cows of the Jersey-Shorthorn or Jersey-Sussex cross, and a few sheep. The farm is now all grass, and since he had come into occupation he had grubbed a piece of plantation and sown it down with grass. He had erected a range of fattening sheds and pens, largely by his own labour, and he had also made all his own coops. He was just thinking of buying a separator to deal rapidly with the milk, making butter, of course, from the cream, and using the separated milk for the chickens. He was also about to try an experiment in crossing the Indian Game and Dorking, as he believed that this ought to produce a good class of fowl for his purpose."

But I may add that the Rev. G. W. Pennethorne, vicar of Heathfield, stated " that three acres and a cow, plus poultry, or better still, six acres and two cows, plus poultry, provided a decent living. He cited several instances known to him of labourers who had risen from the ranks, so to speak, by the aid of poultry."

These facts show that there is an opportunity for development of poultry fattening, and consequently of poultry rearing, in Britain, and thus obviate the need for those vast quantities of chickens, geese, and turkeys which are imported from France, and from such widely separated countries as Russia and Canada. Few people realise the extent to which we are dependent upon foreign supplies of both eggs and poultry. Statistics can be found in my work on "Poultry Keeping as an Industry for Farmers and Cottagers," and need not here be repeated.

The most striking fact in this connection is the predominance of London markets in supplying the best qualities. London is the medium through which passes the produce from the fattening establishments of Sussex, Surrey, and Kent, and the duck farms of Buckinghamshire and Bedfordshire, whence are sent forth the best fatted poultry and ducks. So long as fattening is practically confined to one section of the country this state of things will continue. That there are many parts of Britain where fowls could be, and it may be are, produced as good as in Sussex can scarcely be questioned, but the specimens have not been fatted or finished off. We need, therefore, to extend the system elsewhere, and I hope to see the day when a county without fattening establishments will be the exception, instead of the rule as at present. And I believe traders in all parts of the country would lend their powerful support to the accomplishment of this end. A movement is taking place in this direction, and I hope that it will greatly increase.

The tendency of any business is ever towards concentration, arbitrarily so, and we need at intervals to break it up. Table poultry can be produced in Cumberland equally with Sussex, and ducklings in Yorkshire as well as in Buckinghamshire. Not climate, not soil, not other conditions, so much as brains and energy command success in poultry keeping. The spread of fattening establishments would increase demand for labour, would enable chicken raisers to obtain better prices for their birds, make a local demand for grain and milk, and supply local needs, saving railway carriage and economising expenditure.

There are people, however, who object to the fattening system. They fail to understand it. As I have said before, is it not as reasonable to kill lean poultry as it would be to slaughter lean stock? One is on all fours with the other. Of course, to succeed we should need to improve the breeds of poultry, selecting those with definite table properties, to breed early, to aim for good quality, to study the markets in order to concentrate our output during the time when rates rule highest. This latter point seems to be ignored by ordinary poultry keepers. Remember that when the game comes in down go the prices for poultry. There must also be proper fattening and preparation. It is not what we like, but what our customers want and for which they are willing to pay. I should be glad to see here the same universal skill in fattening and dressing poultry as is found in some parts of France, which I visited recently, where every farmer's wife understands the business, and for quality of fowls marketed they beat the professional fatteners completely. But as a first step we must look to fattening establishments.

How are the changes here indicated to be brought about? Of course, individual effort will be a powerful factor. The example of one success is a great stimulus towards the development of any industry. But we need some means of arousing thought and inquiry as precursors to action. Something has already been done. During the past three years I have lectured upon this subject in about a dozen counties, and in something like 400 villages, under the auspices of their respective Technical Education Committees. In spite of the sneers about teaching with a magic lantern, levelled against those who are trying to influence our rural population in its detail, this work has had good effects, and more will be evident as time goes on. It is necessarily slow, but perhaps none the less sure on that account. A movement like this does not enable one man to make a fortune, but it may help a thousand men and women to add to their incomes a sum which is of distinct benefit to them, and thus be of greater general good.

POULTRY FATTENING.

CHAPTER I.

BREEDS AND CROSSES.

In making choice of any animal for domestic purposes a most important, and, in fact, a necessary, point, is to consider the structure of the animal in relation to the work which it has to perform. It would be suicidal on the part of a horse buyer if he were simply attracted by colour, for he must primarily examine the animal to see whether it is built upon lines enabling it to perform the work he desires it to do. The same is equally true in the case of cows, and this principle ought to be equally laid down for the guidance of all poultry keepers. Fortunately we can divide our different races of poultry into distinct classes, according to their economic qualities, and this is at once an important guide in selection of breeds. Our first point in the choice of stock for producing table poultry is that the bird shall be built in such a manner as to carry a large quantity of flesh in the right place, that it shall have good quality of flesh, be by nature a quick grower, fattening easily, and is sufficiently hardy.

A further most important matter in the selection of table poultry is as to the colour of the skin and flesh, though this is looked at from different standpoints in America and Europe. For some reason our Transatlantic neighbours prefer yellow-fleshed fowls, whereas we always look upon those birds carrying the whitest flesh as being the best for table purposes, and there can be no doubt that the breeder of table poultry who desires to attain the best results must keep this question in view. It will be well, however, just to give a list of the different breeds, showing the colour of their flesh, and this I quote from my work on " Poultry Keeping as an Industry for Farmers and Cottagers ":—

"White-fleshed fowls : Crèvecœurs, La Flèche, Du Mans, La Bresse, Houdans, Courtes Pattes, Barbezieux (a dark-fleshed fowl would not be tolerated in France), Dorkings, Old English Game, Scotch Greys.

" Yellow-fleshed fowls : Leghorns, Plymouth Rocks, Brahmas, Wyandottes, Cochins. Such breeds as Indian Game, Langshans, &c., cannot be called white-fleshed or yellow-fleshed in the same way as are the others named above, but might perhaps be classed as yellowish-white or cream-fleshed.

"Dark-fleshed fowls : Hamburghs, Game, Minorcas, Andalusians.

"Here it is desirable to mention that in Britain there has been a strong prejudice in favour of white-legged fowls for table purposes, it being thought that black-legged fowls were not nearly so fine in flesh. Consequently, with the exception of one breed of Old Game fowls, the only variety fitting this notion was the Dorking. Happily the prejudice is dying out, for it has been abundantly proved that two or three French breeds are quite equal to the Dorking in table properties, and of course there is not one with white legs and feet. The colour of the pedal limbs is not influenced by nor does it influence that of the flesh and skin on the body."

Another important matter is as to the shape of the birds, and the true ideal in the selection of table poultry is that the fowl shall be long in body or keel, broad in breast (giving it a massive appearance), deep in body, and have large wings. Unless the bird is long in body or keel it is impossible for it to carry the same amount of flesh as would otherwise be the case, because the length of flesh upon the breast is determined by the length of keel. Then, again, unless the bird is broad the breast will not give as many slices as is desirable. Third, a shallow-bodied bird must have a shallow keel or breast blade, and therefore the breast muscles will necessarily be relatively thin. The object in recommending large-winged birds as table fowls is because the meat lying upon the breast consists of the muscles which are utilised for working the wings. If the wings are small, the muscles will be relatively small. Nature does not waste her energies, and, as everything produced by her has some definite object, we should acquaint ourselves with her operations. At the risk of being charged with reiteration, it is well to state again what we want to secure the best body : (1) a long body ; (2) a broad breast ; (3) a deep body ; and (4) large wings. These points are carefully regarded in the great poultry districts of France, and in the La Bresse country the length of body receives prominent consideration, a short-keeled fowl being looked upon as inferior.

In making a selection for breeding table poultry, we strongly urge that, as far as possible, heavy-legged and heavy-boned fowls shall be avoided, because, as every one acknowledges, the best part of a fow is undoubtedly the meat found upon the breast, and it is in this direction that we wish to develop. The legs of a fowl are composed of sinews and veins, which are tougher and have less food value than the breast meat, and we should breed as little for legs as possible. A further point is that all feather-legged birds ought to be avoided for table purposes. These ornamental additions to the legs and feet have to be maintained, and this can only be done at the expense of economic qualities. It has been proved again and again that since hock and leg feathers have been so much developed on the Cochin and Brahma, both these breeds have deteriorated in respect to egg and flesh production, and the reason for this change must be obvious to all who have studied the laws of breeding.

A further question is as to the relative weight of meat and bone upon fowls, because in selecting table poultry it is not so much size of frame that we must look to as the amount of actual food thereon. Fortunately we have some tables showing the result of

M. Lemoine's observations in this direction, from which it will be seen that the Dorking, the Game, the Houdan, and the La Flèche, amongst English and French breeds, give us a relatively larger weight of meat than of bone or offal.

The leading varieties of table poultry, regarding them from the higher meat qualities, are :—

>   Dorkings,   La Bresse,
>   Indian Game,   La Flèche,
>   Game,   Crèvecœur,

and, with the exception to be afterwards noted, table-poultry producers would be wise to confine their attention chiefly to these breeds. We should, however, suggest that the French varieties, La Bresse, La Flèche, and Crèvecœur, need not detain us long, as in the other varieties named we have probably greater strength of constitution and they are more easily obtained. But we shall briefly refer to these breeds.

DORKINGS. Of this valuable breed there are four varieties, namely: (1) Dark or Coloured Dorkings; (2) Silver Greys; (3) Whites; and (4) Cuckoos. The Dorking is large and deep in body, as will be seen from the illustrations in my other works, and when viewed sideways forms an almost perfect square when the head, tail, and legs are removed, the chest being well forward. The neck is short and the head medium in size, the legs are clean, and, together with the feet, white in colour, carrying the fifth toe. The Dorking is our oldest pure breed. It has been bred for probably many centuries, and is characterised by wonderful quality and abundance of flesh, this being almost entirely upon the breast. The legs are shortish and have not much muscle. Of the four varieties Darks are undoubtedly the best for practical purposes, being largest and probably having the greatest amount of vigour. Next we should place the Silver Greys, and these two are the best for economic purposes. It has sometimes been said that the Dorking is delicate, but we think that this statement applies chiefly to it in damp situations, as the breed is able to withstand cold quite easily. Our contention is evidenced by the fact that Dorkings are not only bred in the south of England, but as far north as Banffshire in Scotland, down the east coast of that country, in the north of Ireland, and in the hill country of Cumberland and Westmoreland. Strange though it may seem, many of the best Dorkings of late years have been bred in Scotland and Ireland. Dorkings grow to a great size, and a dozen pounds is no uncommon weight for an adult cock.

In selecting Dorkings for table purposes, the following points are most important : (1) that the bird shall be large and broad in body, with a good square frame and a straight keel or breast-bone—a weak breast-bone being met with in many families of Dorkings ; (2) that it shall have good flesh qualities ; (3) that the legs and feet shall be pure white; and (4) that the bone shall be fine. This question of bone has been somewhat neglected of late years, probably due to crossing with other breeds in order to obtain size ; but we should urge attention being paid to it. A coarse-boned Dorking is obviously against common sense. I have been glad to see at some of the shows recently held a number of winners exceptionally good in this respect, and hope that breeders will keep the point in view.

SUSSEX FOWLS. At one time the fowls chiefly found in the Surrey and Sussex districts were much more even in type than is now the case. They were not, however, pure Dorkings, though there was a close affinity between the two, both having white legs and skin, and at once early layers and sitters, the chickens maturing rapidly. These are qualities that must give any breed a striking advantage over others, and for that reason a strong preference is still declared for the older type. Often have fatteners lamented their inability to secure these fowls. To that end a brief description of the Sussex breed may be of service, written some years ago by Mr. Harrison Weir : " The Surrey or Sussex fowl was generally of a grey colour, often a sandy-brown, and brown, like a Black Red Game. I have put the colours in the order in which they were most admired, and in which size was generally to be found. They were large, strong-made, sprightly, good flyers, and excellent foragers, fair layers, with large white eggs; their legs and feet were of a clear soft-looking pinky white, breast more broad than very deep, with much flesh, and also good on the thighs, &c. They were very close in feather, thereby not looking nearly the size they actually were. Some of the breeds were bearded, but these were somewhat smaller. I never remember seeing any with topknots. The combs were single, and the ear-lobe a pinky-white, like the true Dorking."

INDIAN GAME. The Indian Game might with greater

correctness be termed Cornish Game, as it undoubtedly was perfected in the south-west of England. We do not know just how the variety was produced, but it has been a most valuable addition to our English poultry. Probably there has been an admixture of Malay blood with the old fighting Game. It is a large, heavy-boned fowl, but carrying a considerable amount of flesh upon the breast, which is good in quality. The plumage is partridge and very rich. Its legs and skin are yellow, and the legs and neck long, but we should urge that shorter-legged birds be selected for table purposes. For first-class table qualities Indian Game cannot possibly compare with the Dorking, having yellow flesh and legs, and also being much heavier in bone. It is, however, a most valuable breed for crossing with the Dorking, and its hardihood enables this cross to be produced in places where pure Dorkings would be a little tender. Moreover, as a cross generally seems to follow the mother, we mean in respect to colour of flesh and legs, the special Indian Game qualities are not seen so much in the progeny as might have been expected, whilst they make rapid growth and give splendid quality of flesh, and the breed is rendering very great service in the improvement of our English table poultry. We should seek for vigour of body, good size, and well-developed flesh in securing specimens.

GAME. The breeds of poultry coming under this name must be divided into two distinct classes: (1) the Old English type of Game; (2) the Modern Game. These latter may be dismissed at once as undesirable, in that they are far too much bred for length of neck and legs to be useful for economic purposes. Handsome they undoubtedly are, but lacking in the qualities for which we are seeking. We therefore turn our attention to the old-fashioned type of Game—that is, the fighting cocks of days gone by. These birds are short in the leg, have good square bodies, with beautiful quality of meat. Some have white legs, and these of course would be preferred for first-class table quality. There are several colours, and no one can get far wrong—the Black Reds being often preferred, as they are amongst the largest. We have recently noticed, however, a tendency to rather lengthen the leg of these birds, and trust that it will not continue, for to do so will be at the expense of breast qualities, as in the case of Modern Game. Purebred Game fowls are not recommended for marketing purposes. Nothing can be finer for the supply of one's own table, and if this were the object they can be selected without fear. But the flesh is a little too close, hard, and dark for placing upon the market, where something softer is desired. The chief value of the Old English type of Game, as of the Indian Game, is for crossing purposes.

In France the two principal breeds are the La Flèche and the La Bresse, the former of which is bred in Normandy and the latter in the departments of Ain and Saône-et-Loire.

LA FLÈCHE. In the La Sarthe district of France are found many of the best breeds of national poultry, and that is the home of this variety, which is the *doyen* of ordinary French table fowls. At the great Paris shows, to La Flèche nearly always falls the Prix d'Honneur, or Champion Prize, for fatted fowls. It is a black-plumaged fowl, with great length and massiveness of body, lending itself to early maturity, and giving magnificent quality of flesh, with extreme delicacy of skin. It has a neat head, surmounted by a peculiar small horned comb, and, like the Crève, has dark or leaden-coloured legs, which fact shows that the prejudice in favour of white-legged fowls for table purposes has no real basis to warrant it. The La Flèche is only a moderate layer, and is pre-eminently bred for its table qualities.

LA BRESSE. The variety known by this name is regarded as the best of all the French fowls for table purposes. For flavour of meat and tenderness we have never met its equal. It was decidedly in advance of the Dorking which we had on the table at the same time. Some of this might be due to feeding, for the French fowl had been fed according to Gallic methods, whilst the English fowl was prepared in the way which is usually the case for our home market. The flesh of the former really melted in the mouth, and it was a rare treat. This breed is divided into two varieties, namely, the grey and the black. The former, which has really a pencilled marking, is chiefly bred in the department of the Bourg, and the latter, black in plumage, in the Arrondisement of Louhans. Hens of both these varieties are good layers, and very rarely sit. Eggs from the blacks are much the larger, weighing nearly two and a half ounces, whilst the eggs of the greys only weigh about one and three-quarter ounces each.

The chief crosses for first-rate table qualities are :—

> Indian Game and Dorking.
> Old English Game and Dorking.
> Indian Game and Houdan.
> Old English Game and Houdan.

The above give the very best results in table poultry, and many of the leading winners in the cross-bred table poultry classes at shows of late years have been one or other of the crosses named. Of course almost any breed can be improved for table qualities by the introduction of Dorking, Indian Game, or Old English Game blood, and hence there have been some excellent specimens shown of crosses with the general purpose and non-sitting varieties. The breeds we have named may be called the first rank of poultry for the table, as also the crosses already indicated; the second rank would comprise Langshans, Plymouth Rocks, Scotch Greys, and Wyandottes; whilst in the third rank are Brahmas, Cochins, and other of the general purpose and non-sitting breeds; but we fail to see why any one taking up table poultry should not attempt to supply the best demand. It costs no more to breed or to feed these than second or third-rate specimens.

As a matter of interest it may be desirable to give the weights of some of the pure and cross-bred table poultry exhibited at the Smithfield Show, held December, 1894, where was gathered together the finest collection ever seen in this country. Weight does not, of course, determine quality, but it is a guide as showing the varieties and crosses lending themselves to flesh development :—

Prize.		Pairs. Total. lb. oz.		Average. lb. oz.	
First.	Indian Game Cockerels ..	14	13	7	$6\frac{1}{2}$
Medal.	Wyandotte pullets	13	13	6	$14\frac{1}{2}$
Third.	Indian Game Dorking Cockerels (Duke of York's)	18	10	9	5
Cup.	Indian Game Dorking pullets ..	12	10	6	5
Cup.	Brahma-Dorking Cockerels ..	16	14	8	7
First.	Capons	15	14	7	15

Some experiments are being made as to the breeding of La Bresse poultry, pure and crossed, in this country, but no facts are obtainable as yet.

CHAPTER II.

HATCHING AND REARING.

THE method commonly adopted in the great table-poultry districts of England, is that the work of fattening occupies the position of a separate industry, comparatively few fatteners doing anything in the hatching and rearing of poultry. Higglers, as the collectors are called, scour the country for many miles round, buying up such birds as may be offered to them, bringing them, of course, to the central establishments, where they are fattened off. This plan has undoubtedly advantages to recommend it, in that poultry raisers of the district reap a considerable benefit by finding a good market for their birds, which are paid for on the spot and taken away by the higglers, thus minimising trouble to the producers. Many poultry breeders, who go in for the best quality of fowls, make excellent incomes in this way. There is also less danger of the ground becoming foul, as would be the case if large quantities were concentrated upon a given spot. We only know one or two places where there is much done in the way of rearing chickens. When we come to understand the figures representing the operations of a good-sized fattening establishment, it will be seen how large is the number of birds passing through it. For instance, supposing, as an example, a moderate-sized fattening establishment accommodating, say, fifty dozen birds at one time. During the busy season, this means 200 birds will be marketed each week, and half that number at other periods of the year. It will thus be apparent that at such a place nearly 8,000 birds must be dealt with annually, the hatching and rearing of which would be a big operation.

When we turn to France we find that much more is done in the way of rearing and fattening combined, but in that country fattening establishments generally only finally finish off the birds, which are partially fat when purchased, and, this being so, the work is somewhat simplified. Even there we have met with a number of places which are purely for the purpose of fattening, no rearing at all being attempted, but purchases are made from the farmers and cottagers within a given radius. But the finest specimens are, as a rule, produced by those who undertake the entire work. In the La Bresse country this is especially the case, and there farmers' wives are wonderfully skilful, and market finer chickens than do the fattening establishments. As a rule from 50 to 200 is the annual output on such farms, and they are killed, plucked, and shaped by the breeders. It is necessary to make these facts clear, because I am constantly being consulted by people who think of taking up rearing and fattening, but have not realised the magnitude of the operations to keep a good-sized fattening business supplied. Where there is abundance of room and the ground will not be overcrowded, there is no reason why a goodly number of chickens should not be reared in connection with a fattening establishment. At the same time, I question whether it would be desirable to entirely depend upon birds produced there, the difficulty being to obtain a sufficient number of eggs for hatching, and to give the requisite attention to the young chickens. We have not yet arrived at the state of things met with in France, where, in given districts, the birds kept are almost entirely of one type. Thus eggs for hatching can be purchased with greater confidence as to results than would be possible in this country.

I do not propose in this chapter to detail minutely the methods of hatching and rearing, as they can be found elsewhere, but rather to show the lines upon which work should be conducted. If hatching and rearing is to be done by a large number of small people, then as a rule they will be content to depend chiefly upon hens. The difficulty, however, in this case is to obtain broody hens sufficiently early, and to do so needs thinking a considerable time in advance, and the maintenance of heavier breeds of fowls which are more given to sitting than the lighter varieties. A complaint which one hears reiterated is as to the scarcity of broody hens at certain seasons of the year. Where hatching and rearing is carried out upon a larger scale, then another plan should be adopted, namely, artificial hatching and rearing.

At one time incubators were very expensive toys,

but during the last fifteen years they have become a practical success, if not an absolute necessity wherever poultry keeping is carried on, either out of the regular season or upon a large scale. We are presuming here that fertile eggs can be obtained even in the winter months, and to that end it is essential that early bred pullets and vigorous male birds be kept, rigidly weeding out the older birds, or great disappointment will be the result. This is a question which cannot be discussed here, but, unfortunately, hens are not as amenable to reason as incubators, yet the latter would be absolutely useless unless the former could be induced to give eggs when required.

There can be no doubt that an incubator is a most valuable help in the work of poultry keeping, and it may be desirable to discount a criticism which is often passed, namely, that artificial methods must in process of time lead to enfeeblement of the stock. This is absolutely erroneous. Examples could be cited where incubators and brooders have been employed for many years without any ill effects, and it may just as well be contended that cows will suffer in constitution because they are milked by hand instead of the natural method originally intended. The advantages of artificial methods are apparent, and, as showing what can be done in this way, we recently visited two poultry establishments in France, at one of which 40,000 chickens had been hatched, and at the other 30,000, during the year. The natural method is scarcely used at all, and incubators are kept at work all the year round, as they have been for more than twenty years past, or whenever eggs can be obtained.

At both of these places a large room is devoted to the incubators.

There are various machines now upon the English market which from personal experience I can recommend with the greatest confidence. The first position, of course, must be given to the "Hearson," made by Messrs. C. Hearson and Co., 235, Regent Street, London, W.C. This is a wonderfully reliable machine, with an excellent regulator, and it is scarcely necessary to do more than mention it, because the incubator has found its way into all parts of the world. It is worked by means of a lamp or gas, and is fitted with a tank, the regulator being a small capsule whose contents expand greatly when the temperature rises above 104 degrees. The power thus obtained is used for raising a cap and allowing the surplus heat to escape. The machine is fitted with a capital form of egg drawer, and excellent arrangements are made for the supply of fresh air and moisture.

Another machine, also fitted with a tank, is the "Monarch," made by Mr. W. Calway, of Sharpness, Gloucester. This is the invention of an American, and in the States it has been known for many years. It is a well-made machine, and is produced in various sizes, and stands upon legs supplied with it. So far as we have gone it has worked fairly well. In this case regulation is obtained by the expansion and contraction of the water within the tank itself, which is made to act upon a flame guard, increasing or decreasing the light as required. The third machine is known as the "Premier," made by

46   POULTRY FATTENING.

Messrs. Mann, Greenwood and Co., of Bedford. This is a cheaper apparatus than those already named, lacking the finish of either, but in practice I have found it to hatch very well indeed. A very fine machine is "Keay's Incubator," made

Fig. 2.—Outside Fattening Pens (Leeves's) at Buxted, Sussex.

by Captain Tunnard, of Rugby. To this the principle of electricity has been applied for regulation, and anything more effective and speedy could not be found. So far as its arrangements are concerned it is very complete as to the supply of fresh air and moisture.

There is another type of machine, made upon what is known as the hot-air principle, no tank being employed. The oldest of these upon our market is the "Westmeria," made by the Westmeria Co., of Leighton Buzzard, a well-made incubator, and which has at some of the leading shows beaten the record by hatching a high percentage of chickens. It is made upon different principles from those noted before, and is regulated by a thermostat. In this case the eggs are laid upon rollers, which being connected with knobs outside, it is only necessary to give each half a turn and the eggs revolve correspondingly.

Recently there has been brought out another machine, also upon the hot-air principle, which is distinct from any of its rivals. It is known as the "Forester," and is made by Messrs. J. F. A. Roberts and Co., of Lyndhurst, New Forest. It is well made, excellently finished in every part, and remarkably cheap, a machine holding 48 eggs costing only 52s. 6d. The regulator is good, and is made to determine the escape of surplus heat in accordance with the temperature of the egg chamber. The lid consists of a frame in which glass is inserted, and thus all the operations therein can be observed. The eggs are laid upon wood matting, connected with rods, and can be turned with the greatest facility, without the operator touching a single egg—a most ingenious and desirable arrangement. Of course hot-air machines require careful attention, because if the lamp goes out or is permitted to smoke, there is greater danger than with tank machines, and it is most important, though the same applies to all kinds of incubators, that they should be placed where the temperature will not be very variable nor too low.

With regard to the rearing of chickens, the first point, whether natural or artificial methods are employed, if hatching is to be out of the ordinary season, is to have a large chicken-house or roomy shed, in which the coops or brooders can be placed. Otherwise there would be great mortality during the winter months. The chicken-house should face the south or south-east, have plenty of glass in it, be thoroughly well ventilated, and the floor be thickly covered with either dry sand or peat-moss litter. Herein the chickens can run about, and if fed properly will thrive excellently during the colder months of the year. We show here a form of house which was some time ago described in an American publication (Fig. 3), and which may be made any size. It is gabled almost to the ground, has a couple of windows in the roof on either side, thus giving plenty of light, which is an essential to success in chicken raising. In a house of this kind 12 feet long by 8 feet wide six or eight hens and their broods can easily be kept at one time, the hens, of course, being confined in their respective coops. Another excellent form is illustrated in "Poultry Keeping as an Industry for Farmers and Cottagers" (p. 66). Later on they may be placed out in the ordinary coops. As to the principles of rearing we must refer readers to other sources of information.

Brooders are equally important for early chicken rearing with incubators, and the same reasons for one stand in the case of the other. The best brooders are of the larger type, combining sleeping compartment

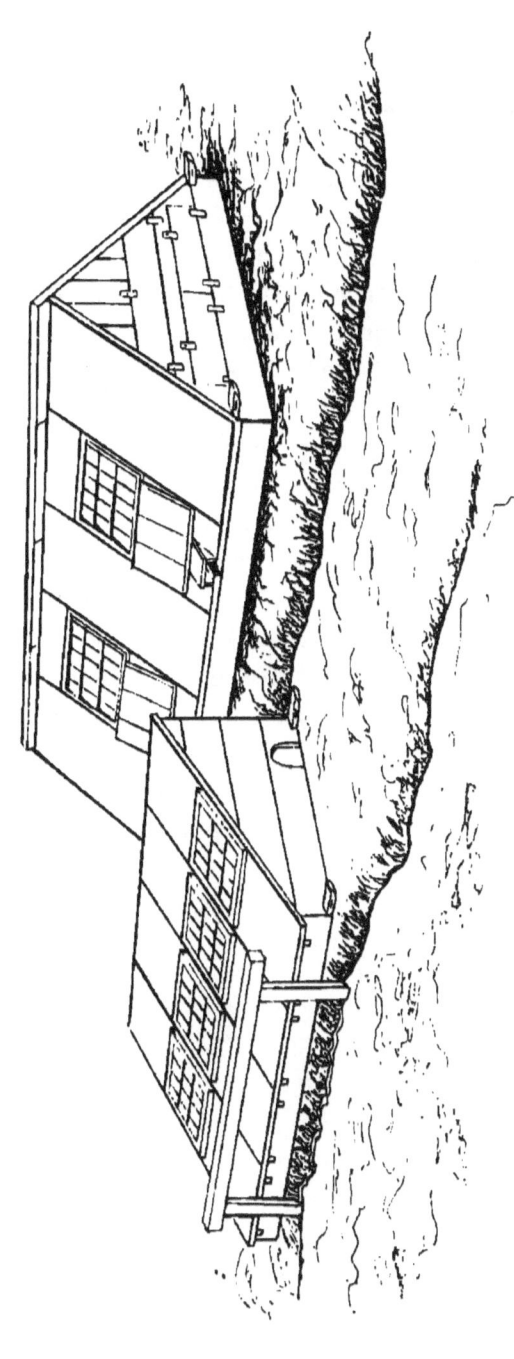

Fig. 3.—American Rearing-House with Chicken Feeding Shed.

and run in one, and these I can recommend with great confidence. They are the "Hearson" brooder, the "Westmeria" brooder, the "Tunnard" rearer, and the "Calway" rearer. Mr. Calway also has a small form of brooder suitable for 12 to 15 chickens which can be thoroughly recommended, and a similar kind of apparatus is the "Cosy Coop" brooder, made by Messrs. T. & M. Wilson-Wilson, of Kendal, which works excellently and is very simple.

At the great hatching establishments in France great numbers of chickens are sold at an early age, say under a week old. These are packed in specially prepared felt-lined boxes, and they can be safely conveyed hundreds of miles in this way. Of late this trade has grown somewhat in our own country, and I expect to see it greatly increase. In the Bromsgrove district of Worcestershire the nailers sell young chickens, sometimes with the hens, and a development of the plan would be an advantage all round, though scarcely so much where table poultry are bred as in the case of amateurs.

CHAPTER III.

SHEDS AND PENS.

It will be realised that one of the first necessities in commencing a fattening establishment is to provide some place where fowls can be kept under the observation of the fattener, be deprived of exercise, and be fed at regular intervals. Various arrangements are made in this direction, though some of the sheds are very rough indeed. When travelling about the Heathfield and Uckfield districts of Sussex, cages are to be seen outside numberless farmhouses, where during the summer season a few fowls are fatted, and when we come across the larger establishments we find great numbers of these cages or pens occupied by fowls, and what would be a description of one place is to a large extent that of another.

There are different ideas held as to the desirability or otherwise of having sheds. In one village we conversed with two fatteners, one of whom had his pens in the open air, simply boarded at the top to keep out rain, whilst the other prefers roomy sheds which, during the colder months of the year, will protect the fowls against unfavourable weather. Given that due attention is paid to cleanliness the latter seems to us the better plan. Of course it can be realised that if a place were not regularly cleaned (and in this respect some of the fattening establishments are by no means models), the open-air pens would be preferable. In many places sun-cages are placed out in the open, usually under a hedgerow; and, in some instances, a fence is placed in front to break the force of winds. Fig. 2 is an instance of this, taken in the Uckfield district. At the establishment of Mr. Oliver, near Heathfield, who is, I believe, the largest fattener in England, long sheds are employed, with open ends, and these are excellent for the purpose, though in severe weather some provision has to be made to cover up the ends. What might do in a warm situation would be inadvisable where it is colder, and we think that in nearly all cases it is safer to have a good large, closed fattening shed. This we may say is the plan adopted in France, though even there the buildings are often by no means so roomy as could be wished, and we have visited places which compared unfavourably with the better type of Sussex sheds. Another disadvantage of keeping fowls in the open air is that undoubtedly they take longer to fatten, except in mild weather, the reason for which must be obvious to all thoughtful persons. If exposed too much in this way the process must necessarily be retarded, they are more restless than when in a quiet place, and moreover there is a great danger of disease resulting from bad weather, though in a closed shed there must be proper ventilation, and prevalent cleanliness also, to keep matters right. One of the best forms of shedding I have met with is shown in Fig. 4, from a photograph taken at Buxted, Sussex. In this case the fowls are kept, during fine weather, in outside pens whilst being fed from the trough, and removed to the shed when cramming commences.

Taking as an example one of the ordinary fattening

Fig. 4.—Fattening Shed (Marten's) at Buxted, Sussex.

sheds in this country, we find that the chief idea seems to be to keep the fowls warm, to feed them regularly, and to have a constant succession of birds ready for the market. We must confess to feeling, in spite of the success which attends this trade, that much might be done to improve it, and the expenditure of a little more money in buildings would probably soon repay itself. Many of the sheds are very roughly put together—too roughly, we think, for the purpose. As a rule the pens are simply made of laths all round, and sometimes the most primitive fixtures are employed. During the slack season of the year labour is generally utilised for making pens. We show here an illustration (Fig. 5) of a better built and well-made pen, which will give an idea of their arrangement. The

Fig. 5.—Calway's Fattening Pen.

pens are about 18 inches high, 20 to 24 inches deep from back to front, and about 36 inches in length, that is, for one compartment, but in many cases the cages are made much longer, and divided into lengths about the size given. In the great majority of instances the entire cage is made of wooden bars, but at one place we have seen iron bars used at the top and in front of the cage. To each compartment is given a sliding door, and it will accommodate from four to six fowls according to their size. Cages of this kind are only built in one tier, and raised some distance from the ground, supported by thin posts here and there. Along the front is fitted a V trough, made of wood and simple in construction, but we think that corrugated iron troughs would be a decided advantage. The drawing (Fig. 6) here given will show the form of pen most commonly employed, and represents the interior of an ordinary Heathfield shed. It would be a simple matter to arrange that the pens be made in better form, and at a very small additional expense, if labour has to be employed, and for open-air pens it is better to make the tops and backs solid. Of course, where the fatteners make their own pens in spare hours, the lack of finish is compensated by reduced cost.

Turning to a somewhat higher type of establishment, a brief description of the fattening house at Baynards, owned by Mr. C. E. Brooke, Past-Master of the Poulters' Company of London, will give an example which offers an ideal, as it is the finest place of the kind yet started in this country. It is probable that the ordinary poultry fattener will have to be content with a less complete establishment, and he would be well advised to build his cages in one tier only, for if in three tiers, as at Baynards, regularity in cleaning is of supreme importance or disease will result. The fattening house, of which an illustration is given as Frontispiece, consists of a large barn, lofty, long, and most suitable for the purpose. It is thatched, and in the midst of the farm buildings, so that it obtains much natural warmth. Windows have been inserted in the roof to give light during the time of feeding, and blinds arranged to cover them at other periods. It is fitted with pens in three stages, each

FIG. 6.—PENS IN HEATHFIELD FATTENING SHED.

bird having a separate compartment of its own. This plan involves greater outlay for cages at the first, but undoubtedly enables the fattener to observe more carefully each individual bird. We have recently seen a somewhat strong criticism passed upon this system of single pens, which is also largely adopted abroad. For ordinary purposes there can be no question that the larger pens answer very well, but the single pen system has manifest advantages. Below the pens, which are made in sets of six, is a long board, similar to that employed in canary cages, kept covered with earth, and the droppings fall upon this tray through the bars at the back of the floor, the latter being solid only half way in. The cages are simple in construction, have

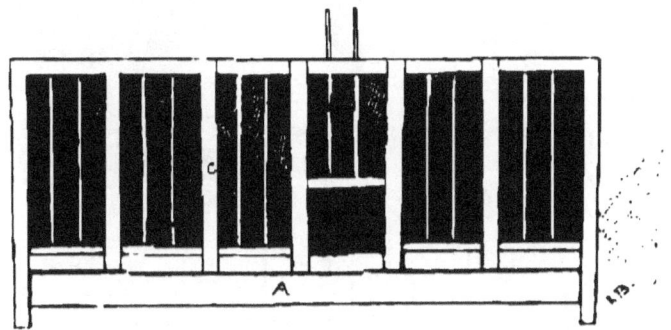

FIG. 7.—FRONT VIEW, BAYNARDS PENS.
A *Sliding Tray* ; B *Door* ; C *Partitions*.

a sliding bar in front, and stand upon short feet. The food trough runs the whole length of each set of six. Mr. Brooke has given me the measurements of the cages, namely—length, 6 ft. ; depth 1 ft. 6 in. ; height, 1 ft. 9 in., divided into six compartments ; the tray is 3 in. deep, and slides easily in and out, and the legs are carried 6 in. below the pen proper. We give an outline illustration (Fig. 7), but the arrangement can be clearly seen in the view of the Baynards shed.

The third illustration (Fig. 8) represents the fattening and killing houses at the French Poultry School, Gambais, near Houdan, France. The fattening house

Fig. 9.—Fattening and Killing Sheds, Gambais, France.

is a good one, and the internal arrangements are not dissimilar to those at Baynards, the pens also being in three tiers. Similar arrangements are made for light, as it is found that the birds fatten better when kept in semi-darkness. Wonderfully perfect table poultry are produced here, selling for two francs the pound. The killing house to the right is a convenient arrangement, and keeps the fattening shed much sweeter, removing the work of killing and plucking—a plan usually followed everywhere. The pens here are rather more elaborate than we use in this country, consisting of substantial three-tier cages, each bird provided with a separate compartment, and the whole made of solid wood except in front, where there is an opening door. Each compartment is fitted with a drawer below to receive the droppings, and there is the usual food trough in front.

The different forms here described will show that there is no slavish adherence to one kind of pen, but whilst we prefer the single pen arrangement for the better qualities of fowls, it is desirable to avoid undue elaboration in any part of the operations.

The following is from a description of the process carried on at a large poultry establishment near Metz, Germany, which I visited some years ago, and afterwards wrote the account given below:—

Twenty-four hours after the chickens are hatched they are removed into cages, fitted in the various upper rooms of the schloss. These rooms, of which there are six, are on the top floor. The cages are simple, having straight lattice fronts, which vary in space between bars according to the age of the birds. Sliding doors facilitate cleaning, and the cages vary in size, for, as twenty birds are kept together, they need more space as they grow. Out of these cages they never go. Before them is a constant supply of food, made of maize-meal and buckwheat-meal mixed with milk, for several cows are kept on the farm. A little phosphate of lime is given for bone and feather formation. Each room is warmed, and yet there is a constant supply of fresh air, but it must pass around the stove ere entering, so that the birds are kept in an even temperature. Treated in such a way, many chickens are ready for killing at six weeks old, whilst all meet their fate ere they attain two months. At this latter age many weigh 3 lb. each, and the prices per pound varies from 1s. 3d. to 11d., according to the season. They are killed on the spot, and dispatched in various ways, the German Parcel Post being cheaper than ours, and so tends to develop business. In summer ice is used for packing. In 1890 9,000 chickens were reared in this manner, in addition to nearly 1,000 sold alive at two to three days old. Several hundred fat fowls of four to five months were sold, but these are reared outside and fattened in cages, on the French plan, accommodation being provided for 300 birds in another building. It is desirable to mention that the establishment referred to was afterwards given up, for reasons which it is unnecessary to detail, as our object is to show the plan adopted.

So far as other parts of France are concerned than those already mentioned, there is not much to add to what has been already stated. We recently visited several fattening establishments in the La Bresse district, where great quantities of birds are dealt with every year. Here the pens are rather better made than those seen in Sussex, being built of thin rods inserted into strong wooden frames, and accommodating from half a dozen to ten fowls in each pen. In some cases we found them stacked three and four tiers high, with boards between, but as the birds are there only fattened for about a week, for reasons which will afterwards be explained, there is small danger of disease in this direction. As a rule they are kept during the colder months of the year in covered sheds, which are warm and comfortable, and it is surprising how many can be so accommodated in a single room. On farms the fattening cages, not dissimilar from those used in Sussex, though single and of a more substantial character, are placed in a dark corner of the cowhouse, which has the dual effect of keeping them undisturbed, and also in a warm temperature. In one instance I found the fattening pens in a room adjoining the bed-chamber. I am bound to say that, even among the most successful fatteners, very little attention appeared to be paid to the question of fresh air, and I should not have been surprised to learn that trouble was caused in this way. However, no indication of evil results could be seen at any of the places visited. In one or two instances the cowhouse was decidedly better than already suggested, and there seemed to be a fair idea as to keeping the cages sweet and clean. The birds are almost entirely in the dark, the object of this being, of course, that they may not be excited in any way. The best place, so far as appearances are concerned, was at Fleuriat, upon a larger farm than the usual run of the country, where everything was done upon a good scale. A special house was devoted to the purpose of fattening, and though the accommodation was small, the fowls appeared to receive better attention in these points. At the place just named they fatten about 600 per annum, during the winter season keeping about 50 constantly in the cages. We have never yet seen any fattening pens in France placed in the open air, and the sheds are usually of a more substantial character than in this country.

CHAPTER IV.

POULTRY FATTENING IN ENGLAND.

IN the days of Arthur Young the counties of Sussex and Berkshire were somewhat famous for their first-class table poultry, but since that time the trade has been concentrated chiefly in the county of Sussex, together with a few places in West Kent and in Surrey. It might, as previously suggested, from this be assumed that there is some special opportunity or favourable conditions in this district to make poultry keeping a success, but whilst it is true that the soil and position are favourable to the industry, there is no advantage it can claim over many other parts of the country. The people of this district for some reason or another have gone into it, and there can be no question that it has proved a success. Upon this point I have already quoted from the Report to the Royal Commission on Agriculture, by Mr. R. H. Rew, Assistant Commissioner, on the " Poultry Rearing and Fattening Industry of the Heathfield district of Sussex," which has recently been issued. Those who know the district will agree that there are many other parts of the country equally suited to the industry.

Whatever is to be learned in connection with English poultry fattening must be from the Sussex district. Of course there is a large and decidedly useful amount of poultry produced in other parts of the country, more especially in South Lincolnshire, Essex, and the Wexford district of Ireland, but the examples to be met with in the south of England are certainly of the highest type, and there can be no doubt that a splendid quality of fowls are turned out by the fatteners in the county.

So far as the question of the trade is concerned it is very difficult to appreciate exactly what is done in this direction, but I find from Mr. Rew's report already referred to, which is later than the estimate I made two years ago as to the output from Sussex, that the trade now represents something like £160,000 per annum. It is to one fact, namely, regularity of supply, that the district can dominate the poultry markets of the entire country. More will be said on this point in considering the question of marketing, but it may be well to mention that a regular supply is essential to the success of any industry. In the majority of instances fatteners do not raise many fowls themselves, but send out higglers who collect from raisers. I show here (Fig. 9), collecting cage carried on a man's back, for by-roads.

It may here be pointed out that the staple food used by Sussex fatteners is ground oats. The reason for the adoption of this food is somewhat difficult to discern, but oats are largely grown in the district, and

I suppose some genius in days gone by discovered at once the method of grinding the oats very fine, husks and all, and the value of this meal for poultry fattening. Certainly the results are excellent, and it is used universally. So great is the demand that millers in the Frant district of Kent lay themselves out specially for it. There is no reason why ground oats should not be prepared elsewhere, and in fact many years ago, when living in the North of England, I used to have oats specially ground for poultry. It is only necessary that the stones shall be sharp and run very low. With the ground oats is used an admixture of fat and milk, the fat being increased in quantity as the process

FIG. 9.—SUSSEX COLLECTOR WITH CAGE ON BACK.

goes on. Mr. Oliver, of Heathfield, sometimes pays as much as £20 for milk in one week during the busy season. We have not heard of the adoption of other foods, though in one or two cases we believe that Indian meal has been added to the ground oats. In this connection it may be mentioned that the Lancashire duck fattener, to whom reference will be made in a later chapter, buys scraps from pork butchers at Blackpool, for which he pays a penny a pound, and these he boils down, giving him a cheap and good supply of pure fat. Similar arrangements could be made in the neighbourhood of other large towns and watering-places. Where dairying is carried on to a large extent there is usually a plentiful supply of skim milk, and it is sometimes difficult to dispose of the surplus. In fact the manager of a large dairy in the North of England told me that he could dispose of a much greater quantity of fresh cream than at present if they could find an outlet for the separated milk. Under these conditions a fattening establishment would be of great service, as skim milk which has soured is just as good if a somewhat greater amount of fat is added to the meal and milk mixture. During warm weather some fatteners use boiled nettles mixed with the food, as they aver that this weed has the effect of keeping the blood cool.

The system of cramming is universally adopted in Sussex. As a rule the birds are first fed from troughs fitted in front of the pens, as shown in the previous chapter, and this is done for about a week or ten days, after which, when the appetite begins to fail somewhat, they are crammed by means of a machine. The old type of Sussex crammer was a very cumbersome affair, similar to a sausage machine, and requiring two men to work. It is illustrated in the chapter on fattening in my work "Poultry Keeping as an Industry for Farmers and Cottagers." With this machine very good work was done, but it was cumbersome, and Messrs. Neve Bros., of Heathfield, some time ago

POULTRY FATTENING IN ENGLAND. 67

introduced a modification, which by means of a pedal arrangement saves the labour of one man, and is universally employed in Sussex. Another excellent machine is the "Hearson" crammer, manufactured

FIG. 10.—"HEARSON" CRAMMER.

by Messrs. C. Hearson and Co., 235, Regent Street, London, W. This machine is coming more and more into use, and the accompanying illustration (Fig. 10) will show its operation. It consists of a reservoir for the food, below which is a pump cylinder. In this operates a piston rod worked by a foot lever. From the cylinder is a nozzle, covered with indiarubber tubing. The food is made semi-liquid, say, rather thicker than the consistency of cream, and is placed in the reservoir. The method of operating is as follows: Take the tube in the right hand, the bird's head in the left, the bird itself being held under the left arm; then, with the assistance of the finger and thumb of the right hand, open the bird's mouth, and slip the forefinger of the left hand into it, to hold down the tongue; quickly insert the end of the tube, and push it down four or five inches (according to the size of the bird); at this moment depress the heel of the right foot (which up to this time had been resting on the treadle), and force the contents of the cylinder into the bird's crop. If the crop be full enough, the tube may now be withdrawn, taking care, however, to relieve the pressure on the treadle for a second or two before taking the tube out, otherwise a small quantity of the food will continue to flow after the tube is removed. It may be mentioned that the quantity of food can be regulated to a nicety, and the great point is to cease the moment sufficient has been placed in the crop. A most important point in connection with the fattening of poultry is to give the food regularly, and if there is any remaining in the crop from the previous meal not to feed at all.

As showing what can be done by the system of fattening, I give some figures kindly supplied to me by Mr. C. E. Brooke, Past-Master of the Poulters' Company of London, showing the increase of weight in the birds he exhibited at the Dairy Show of 1894. Twenty-four birds in all were put up for fattening, nine cockerels and fifteen pullets, and the total gain, after the birds had been killed and plucked, was 57 lb. 3½ oz., the greatest gain being 2 lb. 15¼ oz. in the case of a Houdan-Indian Game pullet. The birds were kept under the process from September 10th to October 8th, a period of twenty-eight days, but the prolongation was for a special purpose. The following is the increase of weight during the process of fattening :—

	lb.	oz.
Gain first week (September 10th to 17th)	11	4
,, second week (September 17th to 24th)	32	11
,, third week (September 24th to October 1st)	8	14
,, last week (October 1st to 8th) weighed dead	2	6½
Total gain on 24 birds (September 10th to October 8th)	55	3¼

This shows that the greatest amount of gain was during the first and second weeks. The average gains during the different periods are of interest :—

	lb.	oz.	Gain. lb.	Gain. oz.
Average weight September 10th (24 birds)	4	15½		
,, ,, September 17th	5	8¾	0	9¼
,, ,, September 24th	6	14½	1	5¾
,, ,, October 1st	7	4	0	5¼
,, ,, October 8th	7	5½	0	1¼
Total average gain over the entire period			2	6

It is interesting in this connection to show the respective gains of the various breeds and crosses amongst the birds used for the experiment :—

	Total gain.		Average gain.	
	lb.	oz.	lb.	oz.
6 Houdan-Indian Game	15	12¼	2	10
6 Indian Game-Dorking	14	3½	2	6
4 Plymouth Rocks	9	2¼	2	4¼
8 Plymouth Rock-Dorking	18	1½	2	4

From which it will be seen that the Houdan-Indian Game came out with the greatest average gain, thus confirming the recommendation already made with regard to this cross.

Recently I have been favoured with a statement from one of our most successful poultry fatteners, as to the rules which guide him, and the methods he adopts to ensure success. The following is a summary of his observations:—

First. In fattening fowls the actual amount of food supplied goes only a little way in the production of flesh, as compared with the conditions under which the birds are kept.

Second. There is considerable difference in the readiness with which fowls fatten, even of the same variety. Large-framed birds, well grown, produce the finest specimens.

Third. Where first quality birds are to be turned out, those selected should be placed in a large run (outside), and for the first three or four weeks fed on no more than one meal a day. They are then removed to the pens, and the food gradually increased in quantity until they have as much as they can eat, when they are finally finished off by cramming, this last stage occupying three weeks. The object of this treatment is to gradually build up the flesh upon the frame. This method is not suitable for young chickens, which are fed right off, and is not usual with ordinary fowls, but for large fowls to be killed about Christmas.

Fourth. When cramming commences each bird should be placed in a separate pen, or half a dozen of the same age and sex may be together, in a quiet, sweet, and, if possible, rather dark room or shed, and for the first few days be fed from a trough, finishing off by the crammer. The food should consist of either fine barley-meal or fine Kentish ground oats, mixed with a little fat, and made with milk into a paste for feeding from the trough, and like very thick cream when used with the crammer. The fat should be small in quantity at first, but may be gradually increased during the process.

Fifth. Before a bird is crammed the crop should be felt, and if there remains any food in it from the previous meal no food is given until the next time of feeding. Observations should be made as to the quantity assimilated, so as to give a fowl each time as near as possible just about as much as it can digest. Should a bird show any signs of sickness during the process it should be placed in an open run for twenty-four hours without food. To aid digestion grit may be given in a dish before each pen, and boiled nettles mixed with the food twice or thrice a week as an aid in keeping the blood cool. Young chickens may be fed thrice a day, but for older birds twice a day is much to be preferred.

Sixth. After the birds are killed, to prepare for which they should be kept without food for thirty-six hours, the blood is drained from the body and the fowls plucked immediately. The meat is then drawn by the hands forward to the breast, and the legs tied back to keep it in place. The bird, whilst still warm, is dipped in cold water,.and thus becomes stiff, but it is an improvement to wrap the body in linen cloths dipped in milk or water.

The above indicates the methods adopted for producing the best table fowls, and whilst entailing trouble and care, brings its own reward, for the specimens so produced command good prices.

In South Lincolnshire, Essex, and County Wexford, the cramming system has hitherto been practically unknown, and the birds sent out from these districts would be greatly improved by its adoption. It is surprising, but nevertheless a fact, that many poultry feeders there knew nothing until recently of the Sussex methods; had they inquired why their fowls only occupied a second or third-rate position in the London markets this knowledge would have been obtained. We are glad to know, however, that one result of lectures organised by County Councils has been to spread information upon this point, and, further, that in some few cases cramming machines are coming into use. Probably when their value is appreciated they will be more generally adopted. Almost any fowl can be improved for table purposes by fattening, in proof of which statement it is only necessary to again mention that large numbers of Irish lean fowls are brought into the Heathfield district every year for fattening, local supplies being insufficient to meet the demand.

CHAPTER V.

FATTENING FOWLS IN FRANCE.

In connection with all French rural observations it must be remembered that France is a country of small proprietors and small farmers, and that even where land is rented farms are moderate in their extent. Throughout many of the departments a farm of fifty hectaires (120 acres) is regarded as very large, and the more general size would be from ten to twenty hectaires. This state of things has had great influence upon the agriculture of the country, for much more attention is given than prevails here to the smaller products. Business is conducted in a less wholesale fashion than we are accustomed to find in Britain, and there remains that old-time custom of producers coming into direct touch with customers, which is only possible when markets are depended upon rather than dealers. And it must be conceded that so far as poultry are concerned French women are wonderfully skilful, though in this respect there are some cleverer than others, as will be the case everywhere. These differences will always be found, and I have had offered me as bad butter in France as is to be met with in not a few ordinary English farmhouses, and that is saying a good deal, though the average quality of production is decidedly higher than at home. But it must fairly be acknowledged that so far as poultry are concerned, the general run of French farmers' wives are enormously in advance of those to be met with at home. We may hope, however, that with the spread of technical education throughout our rural districts, and more especially if the younger folk avail themselves of the opportunities afforded them in this direction, and the realisation of the fact that newer and improved methods may be adopted with advantage, we shall see a vast change within a few years. The signs thereof are evident to the discerning eye.

Although the methods of fattening adopted in France vary considerably, yet as a rule one main idea appears to be prominent, namely, that the birds shall be kept warm, in semi-darkness, and be fed on flesh-forming foods. Other points are largely matters of detail, resolved by immediate circumstances. In some places one plan is followed, in another a different custom is adopted, but the great fact to be made prominent is that the fattening of table poultry is not confined to a few counties, but is distributed all over the country. Of course, certain departments have obtained a greater prominence in this respect than others, notably Normandy and the departments of Saône-et-Loire and Ain, but the fattening of table poultry is spread over a much wider area than in our own land. We cannot visit any of the towns which are scattered through the departments of France without seeing the vast amount of produce brought in to market by farmers and their wives. I have visited the market of Louhans (Saône-et-Loire), when there were upwards of one thousand people standing with produce of one kind and another. True, it was a special occasion, being about ten days prior to Christmas, and the market was consequently much larger than usual, upwards of ten thousand fowls being offered for sale, but at ordinary periods the same state of things prevails to a proportionate extent.

It has already been shown that fattening in this country is almost entirely a separate industry, the birds being reared by farmers and cottagers, and sold to higglers, who scour the countryside on behalf of the fatteners. To some extent the same plan is adopted in France, though it is by no means so universal. In the districts of La Bresse, La Flèche, and Le Mans, I have visited establishments where this system is followed, though in only one case on the same scale as carried out by Mr. Oliver at Heathfield in Sussex, for he, during the season, markets 2,000 chickens per week. French women in the district named above especially, but elsewhere to a lesser extent, understand the fattening of poultry, and my observations show that the finest specimens are produced by those who do not market more than 50 to 200 per annum, the entire work of hatching, rearing, fattening, killing, and shaping, taking place at the same farm. When this is so they are taken dead into market and there sold, either to dealers or consumers, the former purchasing for the Paris and other great markets. It will be seen that where this plan is adopted the profits of middlemen are reduced to the minimum, and whatever benefits accrue from the fattening system are retained by the producer, who, almost without exception, grows the food he gives to the fowls from first to last. To do this, however, needs skill in fattening, and that must be conceded to farmers' wives in the poultry districts. For first-class capons and poulardes fifteen to twenty francs are easily obtained, and I have seen the higher figure paid both at Bourg (Ain) and Le Mans (La Sarthe).

Whilst it may be true that some dealers lay themselves out for the production of the best specimens—and as an instance of this I have visited at Le Mans an establishment turning out about 2,500 per annum, some of which are sent as far as Russia, and all realise high prices, the British Consul there informing me that he cannot buy a really well-fatted bird for less than 25 francs—it is evident that the more moderate-priced fowls are largely produced in this way: Live birds are bought in the various markets of the district, some in lean condition, and are fed-up for about three weeks in cages holding about half a dozen, not very dissimilar to those found in Sussex, but more generally are half-fatted, the final process only needing about a week. In the La Bresse district I have inspected several of these places, at the largest of which they market from 2,000 to 4,000 per week, the greater number from October to February, all of which are sent to Nice, Mentone, and the Riviera. But, it must be noted, they do not attempt to cater for the higher branches of the trade, as the prices range from four to eight francs per bird wholesale, according to size and quality. For live specimens prices vary from three to five francs, the rate being determined by amount of flesh already carried. Of course these figures would not apply to capons or poulardes, but it is seldom that either one or the other are offered for sale alive, and when that is the case they are generally of a secondary quality.

Of late there have been doubts thrown upon the statement that caponising is practised to any extent in France, and I have made special inquiries as to this point. The result is that whilst it cannot be said that caponising is at all universal, there can be no question that it is widely adopted, and all the best specimens are so treated. During certain periods of the year women travel about the La Bresse district from farm to farm, performing the operation at a given price per bird. An ordinary fowl will sell for six or seven francs (I am now speaking of the poultry districts, such as Louhans, Bourg, &c.), but a capon will realise ten, twelve, and up to twenty francs, according to its size and flesh. Even when a capon is not more than one-fourth greater in weight than a cockerel it will sell for more than twice the amount. A capon which I saw at the Bourg Show a few days before Christmas, 1894, weighed nearly twelve pounds. These birds grow to a larger size than cockerels, but at the same time the flesh is regarded as much finer and more delicate. Poulardes are only so in name, as there has been no operation interfering with the ovary. Care is taken to keep them from laying, and their flesh is the finest of all. A poularde will always command a higher price than a capon, even though the latter be greater in weight. That caponising is essential to produce the finest specimens of table poultry cannot be questioned, and to the same extent as in France its adoption should be advocated. The best method of caponising, for which special cases of instruments are sold by Spratt's Patent Limited, is fully described in "Poultry Keeping as an Industry for Farmers and Cottagers."

In France the table poultry trade resolves itself into three distinct branches: first, young chickens, from seven to twelve weeks old; second, adult fowls; and third, fat (winter) poultry. So far as the younger chickens (*petits poussins*) are concerned, they are dealt with fully in another chapter. But the following translation from the work of Madame Millet-Robinet* will give information as to the methods adopted in the other two directions.

"*Fattening Adult Chickens.*—One can fatten adult birds by feeding in the ordinary manner, but the fattening is less perfect, and takes much longer than by means of cages. In all cases it is desirable to commence the process by feeding whilst they are running in the open, and then a fortnight of the cages suffices to complete it. Whilst where lean fowls are placed in the cages, eighteen to twenty-one days are needed to fatten them. . . . For adult fowls it is better to keep them constantly shut up in a run, and above all do not mix the cocks with the hens, not even with the capons, which are timid, and will be tormented by the other birds.

"*Means of Constantly having well-fatted Fowls.*— To have finely fatted fowls at all seasons, it is necessary to fatten in the spring those bred late in the autumn;

---

* "Basse-cour, par Mme. Millet-Robinet," edition 1892.

that is to say, those hatched in September and October. The chickens hatched in January and February should be fatted in the summer; those hatched in March and April in the autumn; and, lastly, those hatched in May and June should be killed in the winter. The September-October, and January-February chickens are exceptions which compensate for the additional trouble they entail, for their price is higher than that of fowls sold at other seasons of the year." In her work Madame Millet-Robinet describes the plan she prefers for fattening, namely, by means of cages, but that need not be quoted, the above indicating general principles.

As to the methods of fattening adopted in France, it may be accepted that some system of increasing the quantity and quality of flesh is regarded as indispensable, and we can be content to accept this without question. The methods followed are: (1) feeding upon flesh-forming foods under ordinary conditions; (2) cramming by boluses of food, or *patons;* (3) cramming by a funnel; and (4) cramming by machine. Without exception the food is always prepared from finely ground meal, hard corn never being employed. Buckwheat-meal, maize-meal, and barley-meal are employed, but we have not met with or heard of an instance where ground oats, the staple food in Sussex, is used. With one or other of these is mixed skim milk, but in several districts of France the "whey" of curdled milk is preferred, and in the La Bresse country the latter is thought to give better perfection in fattening and improve the quality of the flesh. Some of the fatteners are content to mix hot water with the meal, but all acknowledge that milk or whey is better. In one case I found that boiled potatoes are mixed with the food, and from the nature of that tuber its addition must be of great service. In some parts of France fat is added to the mixture, and in others not. It is customary when the older birds are to be fattened to divide them in accordance with their sex and kind.

Capons, cockerels, and pullets are placed into respective pens, as there is less danger of interference one with the other when this is done. Sometimes a fourth class is made, namely, whether the pullets have laid or not. In the case of ordinary cockerels or pullets, three weeks is sufficient time for fattening; but if capons or poulardes, they may be kept in the cages a couple of months.

First: Feeding upon flesh-forming foods under ordinary conditions.—This plan can never produce the best qualities of table poultry, as there is so much loss by exercise, and the birds are not under those conditions to induce rapid flesh formation. As a rule, this system is only adopted by those who sell to dealers, whose business it is to finish the birds off.

Second : Cramming by boluses of food, or *patons*.— This is practically the same method as adopted by the ancient Egyptians, four thousand years ago, as shown in Fig. 1, and it is probably the most general to-day. The food is made into a paste with sufficient consistency for it to hold together. There are two ways in which feeding takes place. In the one, a sufficient number of the *patons*, or boluses, each about the size of a little finger, are prepared, and the operator takes hold of the bird's head, either in the pen or out of it—

FATTENING FOWLS IN FRANCE.

in the latter case firmly gripping it between his body and left arm—opens the mouth with the thumb of his left hand, dips the *paton* into a vessel of whey or milk, inserts it into the mouth, presses it down the throat with his finger, and then carries the food into the crop by running his finger and thumb down the outside of the neck. The process is repeated until the crop is full. The second plan varies somewhat. The operator sits upon a stool, with a lot of the paste and a bowl of milk or whey before him. The bird is placed upon his knees, its legs being held by them, the left hand holds the wings, and he places a small quantity, after dipping it in the liquid, into its mouth, allowing it to swallow in the usual manner, there being no actual cramming. Both these methods are very simple. In some instances a combination of these two methods is adopted. The

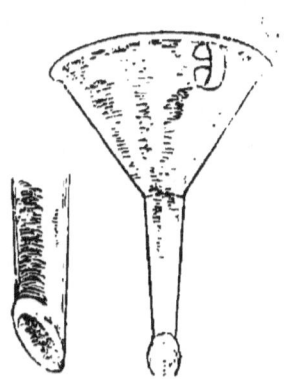

Fig. 11.—Funnel for Fattening.

birds are kept in cages, to which are fitted troughs. After each meal the attendant goes round, feels the crop of each fowl, and then crams a few of the *patons* whenever doing so is thought desirable.

Third : Cramming by a funnel.—In this case the food is made into liquid form, about the consistency of ordinary cream. A specially made funnel, as shown in the accompanying illustration (Fig. 11), the nozzle of which is carefully turned to prevent injury to the bird's throat, is inserted into the throat until the

FIG. 12.—ODILE-MARTIN FATTENING CAGE.

orifice enters the crop, and the food is spooned therein until the crop is full, when the funnel is withdrawn. The quality of flesh produced in this manner is splendid, and I am glad to say that these funnels can be purchased at a reasonable price in this country, as they are simple in use and effective.

Fourth: Cramming by machine.—Several machines are made in France similar to the "Hearson" already described, and their use is increasing; but it is unnecessary to refer to them in detail. These observations would, however, be incomplete without reference to the Odile-Martin system, as adopted at the Jardin d'Acclamation, Paris, and elsewhere, of which an illustration is here given (Fig. 12). A huge revolving cage, holding 210 birds, is employed, built in five tiers, and fitted with a lift, capable of being raised to any tier by the operator. In the lift is placed the "crammer," and as each bird is fed, a turn of the cage brings another into line. When the row is finished, the lift is raised to that above, and so on until all the work is done.

The times of feeding and rules observed are practically the same as narrated in the previous chapter, and need not be repeated. We may mention that in some establishments where liquid food is used, a mixing machine is employed for its proper preparation. In the La Bresse country, buckwheat and maize-meals are largely employed for fattening, whilst in Normandy barley-meal is regarded with great favour. At the Rouillier-Arnoult establishment, near Houdan (Seine-et-Oise), the food for fattening consists of fine barley-meal, thoroughly sifted, sometimes varied by fine

Indian-meal, and mixed with skim milk, or the whey of curdled milk as a change. The mixture is made into a thick cream, and during the last three days of the process an ounce of diluted fat is added for every three birds, or a raw egg to every pint of the liquid used. The birds fed in this manner sell for two francs per pound, and are splendid in quality.

CHAPTER VI.

KILLING AND SHAPING.

KILLING.

THE common method of killing fowls is by dislocation of the neck, and there can be no question that in the hands of an expert operator this plan is most expeditious, and with a very minimum of pain to the victim. It is not easy to follow the method from a printed description, and I should recommend all who intend adopting it to learn the actual operation from an expert poulterer, as it is undesirable to make experiments even with dumb animals. However, as a guide to those who may not have this opportunity, I give a description of the process. The bird should be held firmly by the legs in the left hand, the head in the right between two of the fingers back of the skull, the back of the bird upwards. The legs are then pressed against the left hip, and the head laid against the right thigh near the knee. Next the fowl should be rapidly and firmly extended or drawn, and at the same time the head is suddenly bent backwards, by which means the neck is dislocated just below the junction with the head, and death immediately ensues, as all the large vessels are torn across. The operator must not be nervous, nor yet afraid, but perform the work firmly and expeditiously. Muscular contraction will take place for a few minutes, but if the operation is effective no pain is suffered. To prevent the fowl damaging its flesh, as it might easily do if put down, it should be hung up by a cord tied round the legs, and attached to a hook in the ceiling, or it may be held in the hands. It is always better to pluck whilst the fowl is still warm, as the feathers then come out very easily and the skin does not tear. Regular poulterers start plucking immediately the neck is broken, and there is no cruelty involved, as all sensation is at an end, the head being completely severed from the body. It is surprising how rapidly the work of killing and plucking can be accomplished. If the operator allows the head to hang down whilst he is plucking, the blood flows towards the head, and gathers in the neck, without making any mess.

Unfortunately, in some parts of the country methods of killing are employed which cannot but be regarded as cruel. I have seen the birds suspended by a cord tied to their legs, and a transverse cut made in the roof of the mouth, simply severing the veins. In this way they merely bleed to death, and may take two or three hours in doing so. What the sufferings of the birds are can scarcely be imagined, as no vital part is touched. Such a system is to be condemned, and should be abandoned if now in vogue. A similar way of killing is to be met with in France, where a pair of scissors is used, with practically the same result, though the cut is somewhat deeper. If the fowls are for home consumption, chopping off the head may be resorted to, and this is both speedy and painless, but would be of no use for birds that are intended to be sold.

In France there is another plan followed, which offers manifest advantages to the inexperienced, and I am glad to say that the system is coming more into vogue in this country. For this purpose a special knife is employed, and that sold by Spratt's Patent for one shilling is all that could be desired. It is fitted with a long, narrow blade, sharpened on both sides. The bird is taken, its legs tied together, and laid upon its back; the mouth is then opened with the operator's left hand, and the point of the blade inserted into the slit which will be found in the fowl's mouth. One firm, sharp cut is made right along the skull from back to front, piercing the brain most effectually. To do this properly the knife must be forced right through to the back of the skull, and the brain cut along its entire length. The bird should be hung for a few minutes to allow the blood to drain away, when plucking can take place forthwith. If the operation is properly performed death is very speedy, and there is only momentary pain. Care must be taken, however, to cut the brain as described, or the bird's death will be a slow one. A fowl should always be starved from eighteen to twenty-four hours previous to its being killed, else there will be food remaining in the crop, and this will prevent its keeping as long as it otherwise would, also giving an unfavourable flavour to the flesh when plucked. Too often is this precaution neglected, and we desire to impress its importance upon all poultry keepers.

SHAPING.

There can be no question as to the desirability of shaping fowls in order to give them the best appearance, and the returns obtained by properly shaped birds are greater than when they are sent to market in a rough, unprepared condition. This process partly explains why Surrey fowls look so much superior to others. The system, moreover, is so simple that it can be adopted at a very small expense, shaping-boards being easily made by almost any person. We give here an illustration of a shaping-trough (Fig. 13) recommended by Mr. C. E. Brooke, Past-Master of the Poulters' Company of London, built in three rows, and capable of holding 30 to 36 birds at one time. For smaller producers it can be made with one row, and the cost of material for construction of the larger size would not be more than four shillings. Each trough is made V-shaped, the front of which is rather narrower than the back. One of the best sizes is to have the back board 6 inches wide and the front 5 inches.

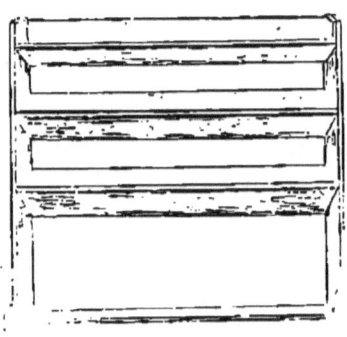

FIG. 13.—SHAPING TROUGH.

KILLING AND SHAPING.

The *modus operandi* is as follows: As soon as the birds are plucked, which should be done carefully and thoroughly, the hocks are tied loosely together, so that the legs are flat against either side of the breast. Before doing so, however, some of the more skilful fatteners draw the breast meat upwards by means of the hands, and this undoubtedly improves the appearance of the bird, though it must be done carefully to

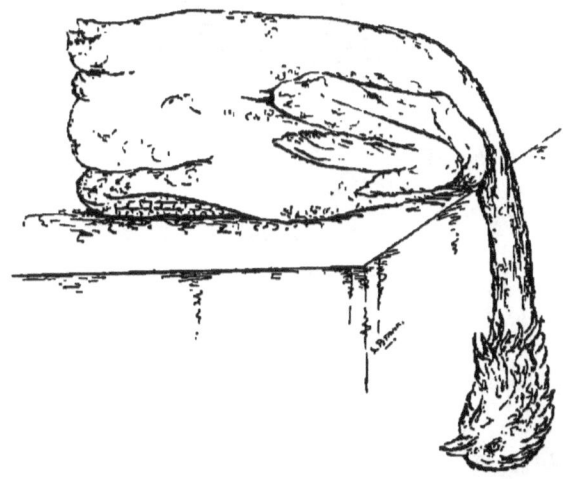

FIG. 14.—SHAPED SUSSEX FOWL *(breast downwards).*

prevent breaking the skin. The operator strikes the stern against a wall, thus flattening and making it fit the shaping-trough more easily. Each bird is laid in the trough breast downwards, with the neck and head hanging over the front. The first bird is pressed firmly against the end of the trough, and a glazed brick or weight laid by the side to keep it in position. When the second and succeeding birds are placed in the trough, the weight is moved along until quite full. It is necessary that they should be packed firmly and tightly together in this way. Next a loose board, 4 inches wide and the length of the trough, is laid upon the backs of the fowls, just behind the wings. Upon this are placed three or four heavy glazed bricks, or weights (56 lb. for preference), and the fowls are allowed to remain in this trough for several hours—in

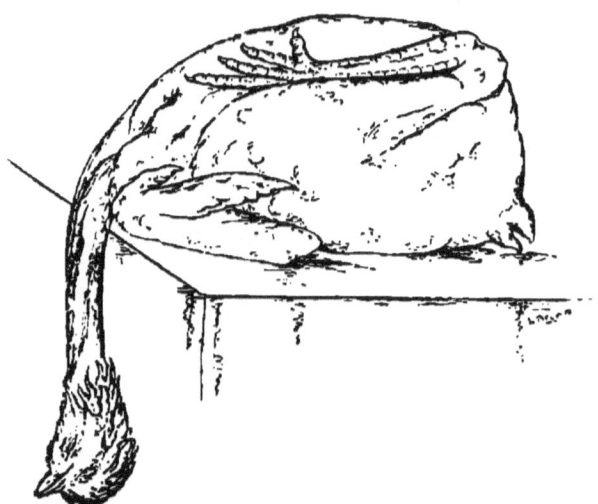

FIG. 15.—SHAPED SUSSEX FOWL *(breast upwards)*.

fact, until they are quite cold and set. When taken out they have the shape and appearance desirable for marketing purposes. What this appearance is can be seen by the accompanying illustrations (Figs. 14 and 15), and we hope to see this plan adopted in all parts of the country. In these matters it is desirable to know the market demands where produce is to be marketed, for " the eye is the inlet to the pocket " as well as to "the soul." We were recently told by a Gloucestershire farmer that excellent fowls sent up to London could not be sold so well as Sussex birds, though of equal quality, simply because they were not shaped properly.

Although French systems of shaping are practically unknown in this country, it is desirable to refer to them, as for the finer qualities of fowls we think they might be adopted in many cases with advantage. The first is that most common in France. In this case a board, from 15 to 18 inches in length and 5 to 8 inches wide (Fig. 16), in accordance with the size of the fowl, is used. At either side of this board, which is usually 1 inch thick, are driven four pegs at equal distances. When the bird is killed it is quickly plucked, and the head, legs, and inner bowel most carefully washed. It is then laid breast downwards on the board, and the back pressed in with the hand, causing the ribs to crack slightly and loosening the breast muscles. When this is done the fowl does not again return to its normal shape, and the meat being forced up on to the breast of the fowl, gives that flat appearance which is so desirable. The hocks have already been tied with the wings through them. When placed in position upon the board the rump and crop are supported by pads of stout paper, or small blocks of wood, covered with cloth, in order to keep the fowl level. A strong linen cloth (Fig. 17), which is sometimes first dipped in milk, and is the length of the bird's body, is very tightly drawn over the back, and the four tapes on either side, provided for the purpose, are tightly attached to the pegs of wood, the head and neck hanging down at one end. The whole is then well drenched with cold water, and left to set. Such

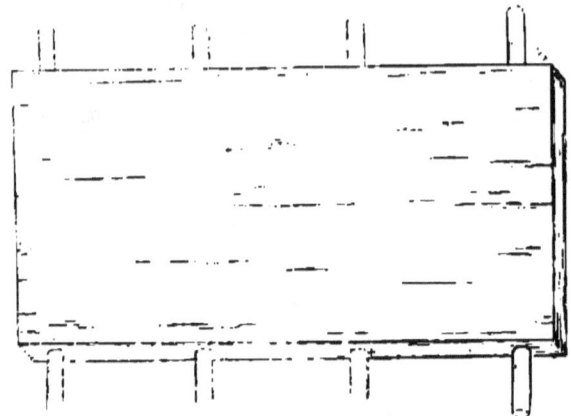

Fig. 16.—French Shaping-Board.

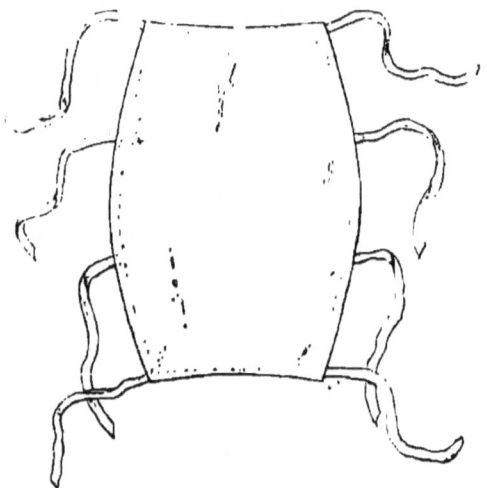

Fig. 17.—Shaping-Cloth for above Board.

a system, though apparently giving greater trouble, is very simple, and brings out all the best qualities of a fowl. These shaping-boards can be made very cheaply, in fact at the cost of a few pence each, whilst the lady members of any household can make the linen cloths,

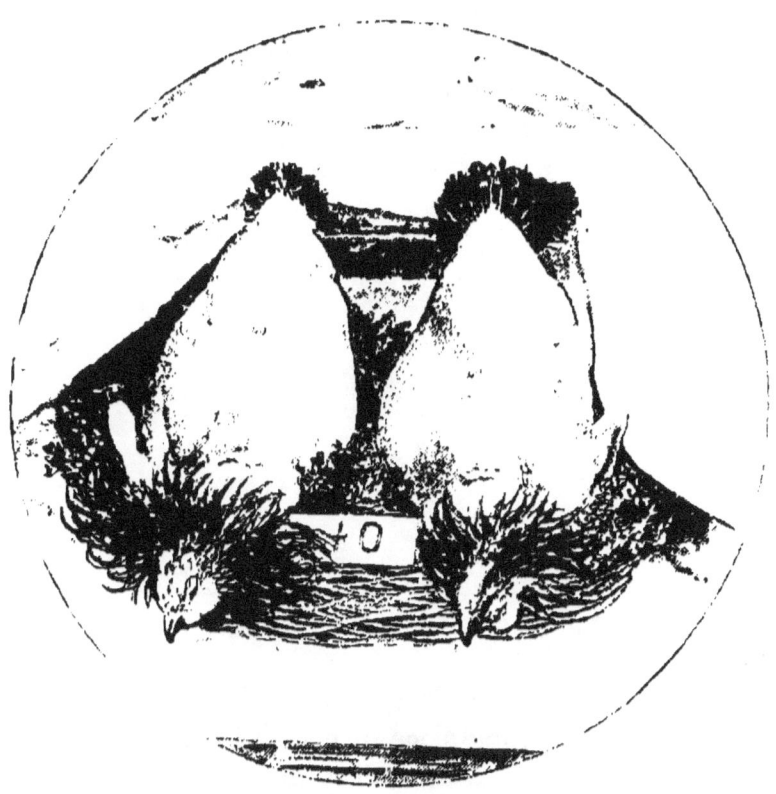

Fig. 18.—La Flèche Dead Poultry.
(*Winners of Prix d'Honneur, Paris Show*, 1893.)

and they are of course used over and over again. Spratt's Patent, of London, supply the shaping-boards and cloths described in this chapter. The appearance of these fowls is shown herewith (Fig. 18), representing prize birds at the Paris Show, where I photographed them.

Another system, which is found almost exclusively in the La Bresse district of France, is peculiar to that country, and to it is due the unique shape of La Bresse fowls. Small poultry keepers and great fatteners alike adopt this method. Every fowl, no matter how small its price, is prepared in accordance with the following system. For this purpose two

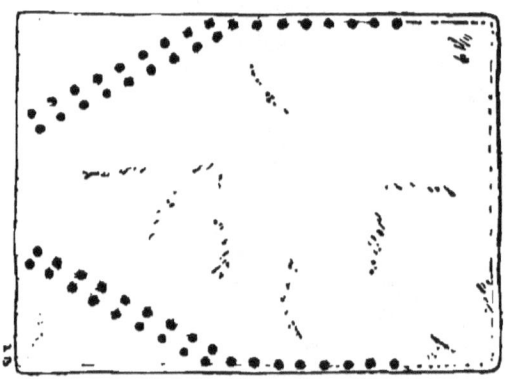

Fig. 19.—La Bresse Shaping-Cloth.

cloths are used, the first a piece of fine linen, and the second an oblong piece of coarse linen or canvas. The shape of the former does not so much matter, but the latter requires to be of a certain make (Fig. 19). The specimen I brought back with me from France is 17 inches long by 13 inches wide. So soon as the fowl is killed it is plucked, and whilst warm, wrapped, first in the fine linen, and second in the coarser material; the latter is then drawn very tightly either by tapes or cords passed through holes provided for the purpose, or is sewn up with fine string. These cloths envelop it completely. It is stitched first from the stern up to the hocks, and then along the body to the neck, the legs being laid on either side of the breast and encased with the cloth. The fowls are dipped in cold water and allowed to remain in this position from 24 to 36 hours. When taken out they have a sugar-loaf shape, the head being at the apex and the stern at the base. The effect of this system is to smooth the skin and give it a very pleasing appearance, as will be seen by a reproduction of a drawing (Fig. 20) after a photograph taken at the Paris Show.

Whilst it is true that the Sussex system first described is probably all that is necessary in this country, still, at the same time, for those who intend to go in for the higher grades of table poultry, we are inclined to think that the French methods here spoken of would be a novelty and appreciated by consumers, though English shopkeepers may be at first too conservative to adopt this view.

Whatever the system adopted of shaping, it is a most important point that the bird shall be plucked carefully, and it is customary in some parts to employ the services of what are called "stubbers." If any of the feathers, and especially the short quills, are left in the flesh, they will, of course, materially depreciate the appearance of any fowl. We desire to urge upon every producer the duty to himself and the industry at large, to turn out fowls in the very best manner possible. Some poulterers are very fond of breaking the breast-bone of fowls. This we think is a most

96   POULTRY FATTENING.

objectionable method, and it is certainly one that ought never to be adopted by the producer. We have often seen a plucker strike sharp blows with a stick

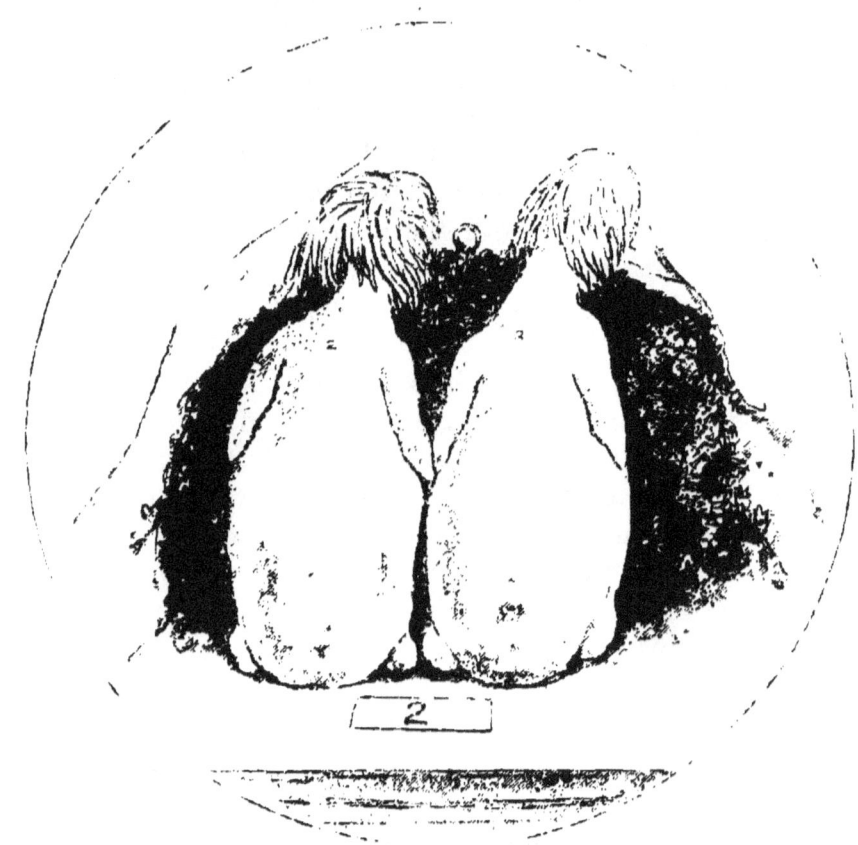

Fig. 20.—La Bresse Dead Poultry.
(1st Prize, Paris Show, 1893.)

upon the back and breast of the fowl, but not sufficiently hard to break the breast-bone, the object of doing so being to give the fowl as plump an appearance as possible. As a rule all Surrey and Sussex fowls are singed immediately after being plucked, and stubbed, and when properly done there is no objection to this custom, as it is simply clearing the skin of surplus hair and feathers. For study of the recognised English market styles a sojourn in the neighbourhood of Heathfield and Uckfield (Sussex), or Boston (Lincolnshire), would prove valuable to a practical mind, and a visit to Wexford (Ireland) and their surroundings would also serve a more useful purpose than many explanatory volumes.

CHAPTER VII.

"*PETITS POUSSINS*" *AND BROILERS.*

IN France there has been for many years a considerable trade done in small chickens, which are found to be in great demand at certain seasons of the year, and sell readily at excellent prices. It may be explained that these birds do not carry a great amount of flesh, though more than would at first be expected, but they are served whole, one to each person, and there can be no doubt that they form a very dainty dish. In this country the demand for them has been increasing, more especially in the West End of London and two or three leading centres of population in the country. Of late the trade has assumed much greater proportions, and we know one breeder who last year marketed about 2,000 birds which realised an average of from 1s. 6d. to 2s. each. And a well-known poultry breeder recently sold a lot of January hatched chickens, when about five weeks old, at 2s. 6d. each. Whilst, therefore, this trade cannot be expected to assume large proportions, still it is desirable that particulars shall be given as to the preparation of the birds, because such a demand will help towards successful results, in some cases at any rate.

The following is an account which was published some time ago in the *Feathered World*, written by a lady who lives a few miles out of Paris :—

"In the department of Seine-et-Oise, near Paris, and especially in the district of Houdan, thousands of chickens are reared early in the spring. They are fed exclusively on barley-meal mixed with milk, or *petit lait* (whey), and killed at five or six weeks old. When dressed for the table, in exactly the same way as ordinary fowls, they are like large, fat pigeons; the flesh is white, juicy, and most delicious. In the swell restaurants of Paris this dish is served under the name of *Poussin en cocotte*. The *cocotte* is a saucepan of brown earth, with a cover (a very ugly thing), in which the *poussin* is stewed, with a piece of fresh butter, pepper and salt. When the little "innocent" is nicely *doré* (browned) it is brought on to the table in the saucepan, and generally new peas are served with it; more generally still this nice and dainty little dish is charged 5, 6 or 7 francs. Not all the breeds are good to make *petits poussins*. Our Houdans are excellent for this industry, as they mature so quickly; they are splendid table fowls and always fetch a good price. This week the market prices have fallen at the ' Halles de Paris,' the arrivals being more numerous; still Houdans were sold from 6 to 11 francs, when ' Couraine ' fowls, which have a great renown, fetched only a maximum of 6·50 francs. I doubt if your English Houdans would be good enough to make *petits poussins*. The breed has been quite altered by crossing with Polands, so as to improve the crest (*huppe*) and plumage, much to the detriment of the quality of the flesh, size, and maturity. This latter point must be specially taken into account for breeding the poor little victims of our greediness. We have in France another variety of fowls, superior to the Houdans for breeding *petits poussins*, namely, the 'Faverolles.' They are bred in immense numbers in our departments, and are preferred to any breed for this special industry. They originated some twenty-five years ago, by crossings between Houdans, Dorkings, Brahmas, and Cochins. These fowls grow to an enormous size, and are splendid for the table; in Paris they are sold under the name of Houdans. Faverolles grow faster than Houdans, but do not feather so soon; the chicks are large, plump, hardy, and very easily reared. Their qualities are their misfortune: they are perfect, and therefore fall victims to those who work at 'the Destruction of the Innocents.'"

As giving further information upon this point, I also give translation from the work of Madame Millet-Robinet, which shows that the trade is by no means a new one:—

"It is difficult to perfectly fatten a chicken which has not attained full growth; nevertheless one can put on flesh and even make it a little fat. In this state it is very tender and delicious to eat, although it has not the same taste as a fowl which has been thoroughly fattened. To bring a chicken to this stage of fattening, it is not absolutely necessary to shut it in a cage as one does an adult fowl. Let it be at liberty, and twice a day give it grain to eat, in addition to what it finds itself. Maize and buckwheat do well. Give them also a paste composed of potatoes, boiled and mashed, and a little pollard, or meal, not crushed. Then they may also have, if the season permit, a feed of beetroot.

"When one has accustomed a certain number of chickens to come to receive this food at regular hours, they run at the first call, but it is necessary to guard them well whilst they feed, or the other fowls will soon devour what is given to them; it is better to put them in a little yard or in a run similar to sheep runs, and which may be composed of wicker hurdles. During the first few days one takes the chickens from the house in the morning and puts them in the little run, where we give them their food; then when the repast is finished they go out, without frightening them by raising one of the hurdles; at the end of some days they run at the first call. In three or four weeks one has, by this plan, excellent chickens for the table."

In order to supply complete information upon this point I have obtained the following particulars from the breeder named in the first paragraph, and also from one of the largest retailers of these dainty morsels in the West End of London, Mr. T. Devereux, of Shepherd's Market, Mayfair. The former gentleman informs me that he has found either pure Dorkings or a cross between the Indian Game and Dorking to be most suitable for producing *petits poussins*, but he intends this year to try one or two other crosses. The chickens are bred as early as possible to meet the demand, and for the first fortnight are fed in the usual way, upon good, nutritious food, care being specially taken to avoid any check to the growth, which would seriously retard their development, and prevent their making good specimens. After two weeks are over, then the object is to put as much flesh as possible upon the chickens, and to accomplish this he chiefly uses Spratt's chicken-meal and ground oats, but every particle of the food is mixed with milk, a little fat being added daily. So quick is the development that upon this food the birds are ready for killing when a month old, and the weights vary from 6 to 8 ounces each. Of course they are kept well sheltered and protected from atmospheric influences, if these be unfavourable to growth. To this end early in the season a chicken-house would be necessary, where the birds would have plenty of room, yet be perfectly sheltered.

Mr. Devereux informs me that the demand has of late years greatly increased, and the period of the year when *petits poussins* are sold is from early in April to the beginning of July. After that time they are never asked for at all. Recently the English supply has grown to some extent, and he, at any rate, does not obtain any foreign birds, except there has been a specially large inquiry, when he has wired to France for a supply. His experience is that English birds are vastly superior to those from abroad. The chicks obtained from France vary very much in size, being chiefly legs and wings, and not having nearly the same amount of breast meat as those bred in this country. As a rule West End customers insist upon all the birds they buy being of the same size, and consequently greater trouble is experienced in sorting those from abroad, as they send all sizes and ages to make up the number required. Upon arrival he has many of the birds smashed in transit, and being stuffed with brown paper to maintain the correct shape, they are often affected in flavour from this cause. Also as a rule the majority of French birds are too large in size. I may here mention that inquiries in Paris have led me to the conclusion that the best specimens do not come over here, but command higher prices in that city, and so, of course, are marketed there. This will explain Mr. Devereux's preference for English-bred *petits poussins*, but the fact is important as showing what can be done in our own land. The best age, in Mr. Devereux's judgment, is when they are from three weeks to a month old, before any quantity of bone has developed, when they prove to be very dainty morsels indeed. The great point in connection with *petits poussins* is that they shall be small in bone, and any variety of fowl which is fine in this respect would be suitable for the purpose, though rapidity of growth is of equal importance.

The chickens should be starved for a few hours before killing, be carefully plucked by the producer, and sent to market packed in boxes, but they must not be drawn. It is necessary that they shall be fleshy, with plump breasts, or will look scraggy, and fail to realise anything like the prices of better specimens. In the months named above the average retail value is from 2s. to 2s. 6d. each. We have, however, heard of instances when very much higher figures were paid for an even lot of chickens. When received by the retailer they are drawn and trussed, the wings being sewn, and a needle stuck right through the body—in fact, trussed more like a pheasant than a chicken. It is usual to place a vine-leaf inside the body, the acid of which improves the flavour.

In connection with *petits poussins*, I also interviewed the well-known firm of John Bailey and Son, of Mount Street, Grosvenor Square, who sell large quantities of these birds, all of which are obtained from Sussex, and Mr. Bailey believes that pure Dorkings are decidedly the best. He does not think that the age can be definitely stated, although about a month is generally the best time for killing. When they are ready for killing they are *petits poussins*, whatever the age may be. In other respects the information given by this gentleman was identical with that recorded above.

It may be contended, as in fact it already has been, that there is a great waste in killing chickens at so early an age, but this we fail to see. The trade in *petits poussins* does not interfere with any other, and is an addition altogether, whilst if the birds are destined to die we do not see that it matters much whether they are killed at one month or three months old. The trade in these chickens can never be expected to assume very large proportions, but it may be, at any rate, one which will grow much greater than at present, and for those who have the necessary skill in early rearing, it will give an excellent return for labour and food employed. It can easily be seen that 1s. 6d. to 2s. for a chicken a month or five weeks old affords an excellent margin of profit, and even though the number produced be comparatively small, yet the returns are quick. To succeed in this, as in every other branch of table poultry, it is essential to breed from suitable varieties, and the best specimens we have met with in England have been of the Indian Game-Dorking cross. Indian Game-Houdans also make very good *petits poussins*.

In America a large trade is done in what are known as "broilers," that is, chickens from six to ten weeks old. For this purpose yellow-fleshed birds are preferred—in fact, white flesh is thought to be decidedly inferior, which explains the reason of that preference for yellow-fleshed breeds which prevails across the Atlantic. The great centre of this industry appears to be Hammerton, in the State of New Jersey, where are large broiler farms, turning out great quantities of chickens every year. Statements have been made as to the extent of this industry, but in the absence of reliable figures it might be misleading to reproduce them. It may, however, be taken for granted that the business done is large, and if continuity of operations is any evidence of success, that it is profitable.

The following notes are summarised from an article by Mr. James Rankin, of South Easton, Mass., a well-known American poultry breeder :—

No food is required for the first twenty-four (or even thirty-six) hours. Then keep granulated (pin-head) oatmeal in a little trough always within their reach, giving soaked bread and milk three times a day, until they are three days old, when they may be given a little chopped meat once a day. An excellent bread may be made for them by combining equal parts of ground oats, corn-meal, middlings, and ground meat, baking the mixture in an oven. Stale bread of any kind, crackers, or other cereal foods are also excellent. As soon as the chicks are able to eat wheat and cracked corn, they will require but little labour in feed, as it will be necessary to give them only a morning and night meal of soft food. The soft food may consist of corn-meal, ground oats, and ground meat, equal parts, scalded; but any variety, such as cooked potatoes or turnips, chopped cabbage or onions, milk or anything they will eat, may be given with the soft food at noon.

Broilers are sold entire, the feathers only being removed. They must be dry-picked, the pin-feathers removed, and the skin free from bruises or rents. Pack in boxes or barrels and ship by express. They cannot be sent to market alive in cold weather, as they would perish. The cost per pound of broiler for food only is $2\frac{1}{2}$d.; but the cost of the eggs for hatching, fuel, and warmth, labour, and interest on investment must be considered in the cost. If well fed the chicks will double their weight every ten days until they are forty days old. If forced, they will weigh a pound each when six weeks old, and two pounds at ten weeks. The space used on the broiler farms under shelter is 5 feet by $7\frac{1}{2}$ feet, with yards 15 feet by 16 feet for 100 chicks. They never leave this space until they are sent to market. The brooder is one yard square. As the brooder-house is warmed by the heat that escapes from the brooders, if the chickens grow too large for the brooders (by which time they are usually well fattened) they do not all go under the brooder.

The first broilers usually come to market about February 1st, and they should weigh not over a pound. Then follow those not over $1\frac{1}{4}$ pounds in March. April and May demand sizes not over $1\frac{1}{2}$ pounds. The prices vary from 1s. to 2s. 6d., and occasionally more, per pound, the highest in April and May. The best market is New York City early in the season, but Boston prices equal those of New York later. Chicago prices equal those of New York, but the demand is a little later than in New York for the early lots.

CHAPTER VIII.

FATTENING DUCKS.

For a long period of time the Aylesbury district of Buckinghamshire has been famous as the centre of a great industry in the hatching and rearing of ducklings. From that vale have emanated birds of a character which has made the Aylesbury duck one of the most valuable we possess. Its special qualities of rapid growth and richness of flesh, more especially the former, have given it a popularity which is unquestioned. During recent years the industry has increased and spread into the adjoining county of Bedfordshire, around the town of Leighton Buzzard, and it is sometimes contended that the more important branches of the industry are now met in the Leighton district. The villages of Haddenham and Weston Turville in Buckinghamshire, and of Stanbridge, from whose station vast quantities are dispatched every year, Eatonbray and Great Billington in Bedfordshire, are centres of large duck-producing districts, and the "quack, quack" of these birds is to be heard on all sides during the spring of the year. The duck fatteners, or "duckers" as they are called, do not as a rule keep breeding stock, but buy eggs from the farmers in the district, who receive a considerable benefit in this way. The amount of space taken up by the actual rearing of the ducklings is very limited. For instance, at Stanbridge, one ducker who kills about 1,300 to 1,900 birds in the season, does all the work upon what cannot be more than one-fourth of an acre. At Eatonbray another ducker I have visited, had last spring 2,000 ducklings in various stages of growth, and from 200 to 300 hens sitting upon eggs. This man has killed as many as 6,000 in a single year. But this number is exceeded by a farmer at Great Billington, who last year killed close upon 10,000 ducklings. From the evidence obtained it is clear that whatever poultry keeping may be in other parts of the country, the duckers of North Buckinghamshire and Bedfordshire find it a profitable business.

In a report by Mr. Aubrey Spencer to the Royal Commission on Agriculture,[*] relating to the condition of agriculture in the Vale of Aylesbury, there is some interesting information as to the duck-fattening industry in that district. It appears that the persons who engage in duck-fattening in Aylesbury and the surrounding villages are generally men of the labouring class or small village tradesmen. The number of ducklings reared and sold annually by individuals varies from a few hundred to several thousands. The ducks, which are always of the large, pure white,

[*] "Report by Mr. Aubrey Spencer (Assistant Commissioner) on the Vale of Aylesbury, and the county of Hertford." London: Eyre and Spottiswoode.

or Aylesbury breed, require constant care and attention all through the spring months, and no one who rears a large number would, during that period, have time to engage in any other work. But where a comparatively small number is reared, the female portion of the household perform most of the necessary labour. Many of those engaged in rearing are said to find time to carry on some other occupation, such as shoemaking, in the autumn months, or, at any rate, to earn a little extra money by harvesting and occasional agricultural work. Mr. Spencer was told that in the village of Weston Turville about eleven men fattened 1,000 ducks apiece annually, and that about 16,000 or 17,000 were sent from there to London in a year. As mentioned already, the duck fatteners do not themselves keep stock ducks, but buy eggs from farmers or others who keep breeding ducks, so that the breeding and rearing are in different hands.

It is a main object of the duck fattener to bring out as many young ducks as he can ready for the market in February or early in March, when the game season is over, and the highest prices are obtainable for ducklings. The season for ducklings commences in February, and continues till about the end of August, the prices falling as the year advances. In February or March, as much as £1 1s. a couple is occasionally obtained for ducklings, and one fattener at Weston Turville informed Mr. Spencer that in 1894 he had obtained the very exceptional price of £1 4s. for a couple, which was the highest figure he had ever reached. The average price in March is stated to be more usually about 12s. or 14s. a couple. The carriage and salesman's commission for the ducklings (5 per cent.) are reckoned at about 3d. per bird, and duck fatteners commonly estimate that, after deducting carriage and commission, they receive on the average about 3s. 3d. a duck. Mr. Spencer, however, is inclined to think that this estimate is rather under than over the mark, for in August, when he visited the district, prices were still as high as 6s. to 7s. a couple.

As regards accommodation, it appears that a small back-yard or garden attached to a cottage affords sufficient room for the bringing-up of some hundreds of ducklings. Some shedding is required for the protection of the young ducks from the weather, and the ground is usually divided by planks into pens so as to keep the ducklings of different ages apart. As a rule, the young ducks do not go into water, but are supplied with water in troughs or shallow vessels.

Contracts are usually made between the duckers and farmers for a supply of eggs right through the winter, and the average price is from 3s. to 3s. 6d. the dozen, but during periods of scarcity 10s. to 12s. per dozen is often paid, and we were informed by one breeder that he has paid as high as 15s. per dozen. Hatching operations commence in October, and to secure eggs at this period young ducks, bred early for the purpose, are mated with older drakes. In this way, as the two-year-old ducks do not commence laying until a later period, a constant supply of eggs is obtained, and not much harm would be done if the ducklings were killed off when a few weeks old. The eggs are set almost entirely under hens, and when the ducklings come out they are allowed to remain with the hen for about a week, kept in small coops, though frequently they are taken sooner from the hens, and sometimes they are kept in the cottage itself. Then they are removed, placed in roomy sheds, which are usually divided into compartments, and must be well lighted and airy. We have seen in a single shed upwards of 2,000 ducklings, divided into flocks of about 25 each by L-shaped boards, so as to prevent overcrowding. As they grow these places are increased in size, and then they are put out into open runs with sheds attached, from 100 to 200 in a flock. On one large farm two long, low sheds are employed, divided by 18-inch boards into a dozen compartments, each of which holds 100 birds. The ducks are allowed out when younger three times a day for feeding, at 7 a.m., 12.30, and 5 p.m., then put back and penned off in the manner stated. They are not given any water for swimming as a rule, but there are exceptions to this arrangement. Water for drinking is given in troughs, which are half-filled with a special gravel brought from Long Marston in Buckinghamshire, and which is regarded as having some special qualities to recommend it. It is inexpensive, costing 1s. 6d. per load, without cartage. Similar gravel can be met with elsewhere, and this material is essential to success in duck rearing.

The food is, of course, varied a little in accordance with the individual ideas of breeders, but as a rule, for a few days, it consists of hard-boiled eggs, chopped fine and mixed with bread-crumbs, but some breeders use at this period in addition toast soaked in water. After three or four days of this feeding the birds are put upon rice, which is properly boiled, and for this purpose Burmah rice is preferred, as it has more feeding in it. Next they are given rice and toppings, which is the local name for fine sharps or middlings. During the later stages of the process they are fed upon barley-meal and toppings, and finally upon barley-meal and fine greaves, or tallow scrap cake, or boiled rice mixed with greaves, though on one farm horseflesh and mutton are used for the same purpose. It is customary to give boiled nettles mixed with the food at various stages of their growth, this having been found most helpful in keeping the blood cool.

As might be expected under such wholesale conditions, deaths are by no means infrequent, and there is in this respect a good deal of difference in accordance with the seasons, but we are informed by one who breeds very largely, that upon the average he was enabled to market 85 per cent. of the ducklings hatched, which seems to be an excellent proportion. One of the greatest troubles met with is what is known as "soft bill." Where this is present the young ducklings are unable to break their way out of the shell, or even if they succeed in doing this, they die at an early age. High feeding may cause this trouble after the birds are hatched, but we think the chief cause is in-and-in breeding, and the use of immature stock. Strange though it may seem, even in the duck-breeding districts, attention is not paid as it ought to be to the use of well-grown breeding stock, and to the systematic introduction of fresh blood. Several obvious laws in breeding are neglected by those whose interest it must be to keep them prominently in mind.

These birds grow very rapidly, and what are known as ducklings, that is, birds that are killed before they have cast their first feathers, are ready for market in about from seven to nine weeks, when they weigh 4lb. to 5lb., and this is undoubtedly the most profitable part of the business. There is, however, a number kept until they are fourteen or fifteen weeks old, when they scale much more, but do not realise so much as younger specimens. The object is to get them marketed as rapidly as possible. The season lasts from February to July, that is, when game is out of season, and a visit to the district after June would show that it was almost entirely denuded of ducks, save those retained for breeding purposes. Ducklings do not receive any special shaping, but if packed tightly they assume that flat form usually seen. The prices obtained vary in accordance with the season, and the following are prices for well-grown ducklings given me by Messrs. Brooke Bros.: January, 6s. to 10s. per couple; February, 6s. 6d. to 11s.; March, 9s. to 18s.; April, 7s. to 12s.; May, 6s. to 8s.; and June, 5s. to 7s. The kind of duck bred in Buckinghamshire and Bedfordshire, without exception, is the Aylesbury, no other equalling it for rapid growth and flesh properties.

Artificial methods of hatching have not been adopted in the ducking districts, chiefly from indisposition to adopt new methods, and hens, of a large, roomy type, are employed for the work. Full particulars of this system are given in the author's book " Poultry Keeping as an Industry for Farmers and Cottagers."

The question is frequently asked, when reference is

made to the duck industry of Buckinghamshire and Bedfordshire, whether there is not some special climatic or soil influence in that part of England which gives it an advantage in this direction. In reply it may be stated that there are hosts of other places in different parts of the country where ducks could be produced as easily and successfully. We were some time ago having a chat with one of the leading Manchester poultry dealers, and were considerably astonished to learn that for some time the best ducks he had received were not, as formerly, from the Aylesbury district, but from the neighbourhood of Fleetwood, in North Lancashire. He went on to state that ducklings of prime quality were obtained thence in the spring weighing 5lb. each, and that in the summer, when the ducks are four to six months old, they sometimes run as much as 3lb. more than the ordinary market specimens. We, therefore, took the earliest opportunity of learning more as to the place where these ducks are produced, and the methods there adopted.

It was at Bourne Hall, near Fleetwood, occupied by Mr. Walsh, that we came across the duck farm, and that gentleman received us with the greatest courtesy, showing us round, and freely explaining his system. It is not a place which at first sight would appear to be the best for the work, as the aspect is north-west, looking over Morecambe Bay, the soil and atmosphere moist, and, of course, much exposed, as the land is low. The moisture is no disadvantage, rather the reverse, for ducks are waterfowl and can do with a much damper soil than can ordinary poultry, though it is a fact that as a rule the finest eggs are produced near the coast line, for what reason has not yet been explained. At Bourne Hall Mr. Walsh farms about 300 acres.

A large number of ducklings are bred by Mr. Walsh, and his breeding stock are to be found in different parts of a very large, sheltered, and shady orchard, where they have full liberty and live under those conditions which these birds so much love. When the land becomes foul, as it does after a time, he removes them to another part and gives it rest for a season. But a further advantage is seen in the splendid growth of grass, greatly relished by cattle, for Mr. Walsh is a breeder and feeder of both horses and stock. The demand for ducklings and ducks, however, has grown so much that not nearly enough can be produced at Bourne Hall, and youngsters are purchased as far as possible in the district, though even this supply has to be supplemented by Irish, bought simply to be prepared and fatted off.

Hatching is almost entirely carried on by means of incubators, which are of Mr. Walsh's own make, and of these he has eight, each capable of holding from 100 to 200 eggs at a time. They are simple in construction and easily worked, and from what we could learn have proved most successful, the average hatchings being about 80 per cent. The heat is maintained by means of oil lamps, in which White Rose oil is used, and the cost of maintenance is about 1d. per egg for the four weeks necessary to complete the process. Regulation is obtained by a simple lever contrivance fitted to a glass tube filled with quicksilver and spirit, and we were assured that they work excellently, though probably something is due to the operator who understands his machines, knows just how they should be treated—and does it.

So far as the ordinary breeding ducks are concerned there is not much to say respecting them, as they are almost entirely of the Aylesbury type, though we thought here and there could be noted a trace of Pekin blood, but that is scarcely to be wondered at when there is so much about. The Aylesbury, as elsewhere, is found to be the most easily fatted, and their quality of rapid maturity is again evidenced.

In the Bucks and Beds duck-feeding centres large quantities of tallow greaves are used for mixing with meal to feed the birds, but Mr. Walsh adopts another system, and so far as the results are concerned with evident advantage. His food consists chiefly of ground oats, but instead of the tallow greaves he obtains from pork butchers in the neighbouring town, Blackpool, their surplus fat, for which he pays them one penny per pound, and there can be no question that this is much finer and better than the scrap cake from candle makers and tallow refiners ; while the cost is, if anything, rather less. He knows what he is getting, which is not always the case with the other stuff. It, however, has to be prepared, and is melted in a boiler kept for the purpose, and when strained is run into large bacon-boxes. We may mention that the Sussex chicken fatteners use fat very similar to this, and when sweet and good it can be thoroughly recommended. The ground oats and fat are mixed to a proper consistency, and fed to the ducklings twice or thrice a day, and as their main object seems to be eating, they rapidly dispose of the food, to the manifest advantage of both themselves and their owner. Under such treatment it is not to be wondered at that they turn out juicy and plump, and are rapidly ready for market. The chief demand is from Manchester during the spring, and Blackpool in the summer, that favourite watering-place being able to absorb almost anything in the way of food.

All the birds fatted at Bourne Hall are killed on the spot, and so rapid is the process that they can be killed at noon, plucked and packed, and arrive in Manchester, fifty miles away, at nine o'clock the same evening. The cost of carriage to Manchester is by no means so great as might be imagined, namely, one penny per bird, the Railway Company providing hampers. Whether there are special circumstances bringing this low rate about or not we cannot say, but it is evident that the Railway Company are desirous of encouraging the traffic. From what we were informed by Mr. Walsh, he has met with no special difficulties other than those incident from every business, and he is satisfied with what he has already accomplished.

Recently an account was published in the "Country Gentleman," of Albany, N.Y., of a place in Pennsylvania, U.S.A., where 12,000 ducks are produced annually. Here the eggs are hatched in incubators, which are set in operation as soon as there is a complement of eggs to fill a machine. On a well-managed duck farm the ducklings should begin to peep about the 1st of February, and the incubators are kept running until about the 1st of July. The ducks are reared under artificial brooders in their houses and in small yards, and not allowed access to water for bathing until a month old. In winter they never go out of their yards until killed. From the time they are hatched until ready for market the ducklings are fed upon all the wholesome food they can digest, and at ten weeks old dress about 10 lb. the pair.

As showing what can be done by feeding, the following may give an idea, namely, celery-fed ducks. These ducks, if forced quickly, are like rapidly grown lettuce and radishes—very tender. Their market was originally made on this tender, fat condition, without the use of celery to add to their flavour. Mr. Rankin of Massachusetts claims to have introduced them on the market. Fifteen years ago, he says, the strong flavour of ordinary ducks put them in the category of second-rate poultry, and he had difficulty at first in selling 1,500 in the course of a year on the Boston market. They are now known in New York markets as Boston ducks. The wholesome food, of course, changed the quality of their flesh, and now the supply is not equal to the demand. They are fed with celery finely cut and mixed with their food for probably a month previous to killing. There is no distinct taste of celery in the flesh, but its union with the natural qualities of the duck imparts a flavour that is simply delicious—little, if any, inferior to the celebrated canvassbacks, which feed on wild celery. The guinea-fowl has lost probably fewer of its peculiar flesh qualities by domestication than any other fowl, and a guinea-fowl two-thirds grown is a great delicacy, but it is not to be compared with a well-grown, celery-fed duck.

CHAPTER IX.

FATTENING GEESE.

The goose industry is one which has been known for several centuries in this country, and the following quotation is taken from "The English Husbandman," by Gervasse Markham, first published in 1615: "Now for the fattening of elder geese, which are those which are five or six months old, you shall understand that after they have in the stubble fields, and during the time of harvest, got into good flesh, you shall then chuse out such Geese as you will feeded, and put them in severall pennes which are close and darke, and there feeded them thrice a day with good store of Oates, or spelted Beanes, and give them to drink water, and Barley-meale mixt together, which must evermore stand before them, this will in three weekes feeded a Goose so fatte as it is needfull."

As is well known the goose industry resolves itself into two distinct branches, and the varieties fortunately meet the requirements in this respect, namely, the White or Embden, and the Grey or Toulouse, these being chiefly used, though of course there are frequent crosses between the two. Embdens are much the more rapid in growth, and are consequently, like the Aylesbury in ducks, ready for marketing at an earlier period, the Toulouse not laying on flesh until further advanced. One leading goose-breeder some time ago wrote: " Toulouse goslings grow bone very fast, and, being loose in skin, they soon fill the eye and the exhibition pen, but they are very deceptive weighers when young and raw ; even under favourable circumstances many strains of them will not gather flesh and fat until fully matured, when they can be fed to an enormous size and weight, unsurpassed or unequalled by any other variety. They are, therefore, not so well adapted for early maturity, and are seldom fit for the table before Christmas, previous to which they dress very loose and blue in appearance, and are quite out of season as Green or Michaelmas geese. Used, however, as a cross with any other variety of goose the produce mature and fatten very rapidly."

From this it will be seen how necessary it is to keep in mind the economic qualities of geese, as well as the other branches of live stock. Whilst there are several districts of England where geese are bred to a considerable extent, notably Lincolnshire and Cumberland, and, of course, the same is true of Ireland, whose quantities of this fowl probably exceed the other three kingdoms put together, there can be no doubt that the finest come to us from East Anglia, by which term is embraced the counties of Norfolk, Suffolk, and Cambridgeshire. In these districts many small farmers look to pay their rent from the geese and turkeys raised, but the feeding and management is as a rule left to their wives and daughters. At one time the size was small, geese weighing, when drawn and trussed, 10 lb. to 12 lb.; but, thanks to the attention given and the greater care evinced in breeding, larger birds are now obtained. Last Christmas Eve the average price in Norwich market was 1s. 1d. per lb. This was for well-dressed birds, drawn and trussed—in fact, ready for the table.

Geese are probably amongst the most easy fowls to rear, and if they have passed their first stages will obtain the greater proportion of their food, more especially after harvest, when they are amongst the best gleaners to be found. The method of fattening is a very simple one. They should be put into a good-sized shed littered with straw; this should be in a quiet place, and away from the sound of any birds which are being kept for stock. Unlike turkeys, they should not be allowed to see the outside, though in some cases an open yard is arranged where the birds are fed. They should be put up about three weeks before being killed, as very often they will not begin eating for a week afterwards. They should be fed on soft food in the morning and corn in the afternoon, a large trough of clean water being always at hand, but not so that they can get into it. The soft food may consist of barley-meal, mixed with Indian-meal and pollard, and the corn of wheat and barley, which are better if steeped. Plenty of grit should always be provided for geese, both old and young.

The following quotation as to the method of killing geese, written by Mr. J. S. Rawson, is from my work on " Poultry Keeping as an Industry for Farmers and Cottagers ":—

"Before killing a goose, it must be kept without food for at least twelve hours, though fifteen to eighteen hours will do no harm; this clears the crop of all food, a very necessary point to be attained. Having fasted the goose for the time required, the next part of the business is to kill it as expeditiously as possible. There are two or three ways of accomplishing this, but the best is by piercing the brain with a knife. Secure the bird's legs with a piece of twine, and then feel for the correct spot at which to insert the knife. At the base of the skull, and at the point where the head is joined to the neck, will be found a hollow place without any bone to protect it; here is the vulnerable point. Now hold up the bird by the legs, and with a stick or short piece of wood, give it a smart blow at the back of the head, thereby rendering it unconscious. It must now be laid between the knees, the head being grasped in the left hand, bill down, and neck somewhat bent, so as to get a better chance of finding the base of the skull. This having been done, a sharp-pointed knife is inserted in the hollow place before mentioned, and a quick stab or cut is given. If this is properly done, one of the chief arteries is severed, and the bird quickly bleeds to death; care being taken that in the meantime it is firmly held, and prevented from throwing the blood over its feathers or the clothes of the operator. As to the time for plucking, that is a matter on which opinions differ, some people preferring to do it at once, whilst others aver that it is better policy to let the bird grow quite cold before it is taken in hand. In the former case the feathers will be found to come out much more readily, and the time occupied in plucking thereby very considerably diminished; but, on the other hand, the skin and flesh being more tender, greater care is required during the operation to prevent the membrane being torn. The usual plan is to leave the head unplucked, and thus let it act as a signboard to tell the nationality of the bird, whether it be a large duck or a small goose. Great care should be taken of the feathers, and these ought to be separated into three lots, the first containing down only, the second small and fine feathers, and the third division strong quills. The latter may be peeled, and the feathers afterwards mixed with those of the second division."

If the poulterer requires the geese ready trussed, as is not unfrequently the case, the following is the method to be observed:—

"After plucking the goose, it must be carefully singed, drawn and wiped out with a damp cloth. Then cut off the neck as near the back as can be done, leaving the skin long enough to be drawn over the stump. Next cut off the feet at the first joint, and do the same with the wing pinions. To make the bird look plump, press in the breast-bone, and run a small skewer through the lower part of each wing. Now draw up the legs, and skewer them through the centre, into the body; when this is done, two more small skewers are needed to complete operations by fixing the shank of each leg to the side bones. It is now in proper shape for the spit, the only thing that requires doing being to cut off the vent and make a hole large enough to pass the rump through, in order to keep in the seasoning when served at table. The goose should now be laid upon a stone or marble slab, and if the dressing has been done shortly after killing, it will be necessary to allow it to stiffen and cool before packing for market. To improve the colour of the flesh it is a good plan to wrap it in a cloth which has been dipped in milk, and afterwards wrung nearly dry. Geese, and in fact every kind of poultry, ought to be killed at least twenty-four hours before they are packed to go away, and great care should be exercised in the latter operation, in order to prevent bruises or disfigurement of any sort. In following the above directions, the giblets must not be overlooked. These delicacies should be put on one side, together with the liver and gizzard, and sent along with the goose to the poulterers."

The following account of the method of fattening geese in France is translated from the work of Madame Millet-Robinet, and will prove interesting to English readers :—

"The goose is of all fowls that which fattens the best and most easily. It is not necessary to fatten geese later than in November, because when the breeding season arrives they do not fatten well. One should begin in August. Before actually commencing the process it is necessary to prepare them by good food, so that they may be well fleshed. To do this, on returning from the fields they should be given some cheap grain, such as buckwheat, oats or maize, and make them dabble in water, to which has been added a little ordinary flour or pollard. Growing beetroots prepare them well for fattening, and are an inexpensive food. One then puts the geese into the stubble fields, where they find a sufficient quantity of grain. When they are in a good condition it is necessary to confine them, that is to say, to place them in a dark shed, quiet and healthy, and above all deprive them of all diversion.

"If one sells the geese dead, the best plan is to pluck them under the stomach before putting up to fatten, because they dirty their feathers in sleeping on the ground; but if they are to be sold alive, they must not be plucked, as they would be disfigured and reduce their price; in this case double care should be taken to give them a clean litter.

"During the first week of fattening they should have only oats to eat, and have water whitened with flour to drink. This food is supplied in little wooden troughs, narrow, and a hollow, long enough for the goose to reach from one side to another without difficulty. These troughs are inexpensive, and preferable to the round dishes in which one generally gives food to geese, and around which they scramble, sometimes fighting so as to reach the food before their comrades, which greatly hinders the process of fattening. Feeding over, the troughs are removed, so that the geese may sleep and digest their food.

"Fattening may be completed entirely in this way, and 20 litres of oats per head is sufficient; but it is long, and although it appears less expensive, it is as much so as fattening done with more nutritious food; besides geese fed only with oats, and 20 litres at a time, do not reach that perfect state of fattening which makes them very plump—one might say, almost incapable of standing upright. After six or seven days' feeding on oats, boiled potatoes should be added, being mixed with the grain and curdled milk ; five or six days' afterwards a little barley-meal, buckwheat, or maize may be mixed with it, or peas cooked or crushed, boiled radishes, &c., and one may give them to drink curdled milk mixed with pollard. After eighteen or twenty days of this treatment, from the day on which they were confined, they are perfectly fattened, and this method is not costly. If one wishes to make them still more perfect, after feeding, the poultry woman takes the goose between her knees, and makes it swallow, twice a day, seven or eight patons made with meal and potatoes."

CHAPTER X.

FATTENING TURKEYS AND GUINEA-FOWLS.

TURKEYS.

In these days size is all important in the production of turkeys. Whilst there is always a fair demand for smaller birds, this demand is at low prices, and if we desire to obtain anything like the best rates, we must have big, well-developed specimens, and the bigger they are the more can be obtained for them per lb. At the Bishop's Stortford Table Poultry Show, promoted by Sir Walter Gilbey, Bart., held December 21, 1893, a Cambridge turkey was exhibited weighing 33 lb. dead, and this sold for £5, rather more than 3s. per lb.—a fancy price, it is true, but indicating the desirability of producing large birds. Moreover, in a London retail poulterer's catalogue some time ago were published the prices of turkeys about Christmas (and I have met with very similar figures in Paris), as follows:—

	s.	d.	
Turkeys under 10 lb. weight	0	10	per lb.
,, 10 to 16 ,,	1	3	,,
,, 16 ,, 20 ,,	1	6	,,
,, over 20 ,,	1	9	,,

Of course, these are the best West-end rates, and for

the finest specimens. It is necessary to point out that such prices as these could not be expected by the producer, who would probably obtain a regular rate per lb. for all his birds, large or small, the retailer dividing them up, and making the best he possibly can of them. But for good, well-grown turkeys 1s. 1d. to 1s. 3d. can be and is frequently obtained. If they were small those figures would be considerably reduced.

For some years the Bronze American turkey has come into great favour, by reason of its large size, cocks sometimes scaling at 40 lb. and upwards. It will thus be seen that by securing large specimens they meet the market demand just referred to. At the same time we do not think they have the quality of, say, the Black Norfolk, which is one of the finest for flavour of any turkey known, but the latter are rather delicate, and hence the greater vigour imparted by the American is a manifest advantage. The Cambridge Bronze appears to be resultant from a cross between the Norfolk and American, and it is a large, fleshy bird, good in quality and quantity of flesh. White turkeys, which are found chiefly in Southern Europe, are fine in flavour, but smaller than our native breeds.

East Anglia, as a rule, produces the finest turkeys, and geese also, as was mentioned in our last chapter. In the majority of cases the farmers' wives and daughters look after the poultry, and as a rule the work is well done. Too often, however, even in these counties, the question of size is not fully appreciated, but of late years there has been a decided improvement in this respect, and much larger stock birds are being employed. The fact already mentioned as to greater prices per pound, following upon increased weight, is a most powerful incentive in this direction. As much as 1s. 6d. per lb. is often obtained for all turkeys averaging 25 lb. and upwards when dressed. The average price in Norwich market on Christmas Eve (1894) was 1s. 2d. to 1s. 3d. per lb. for turkeys well dressed, drawn, and trussed—in fact, ready for cooking.

The sight afforded in Norfolk of large flocks of both geese and turkeys roaming about on the stubbles after harvest, doing pretty much as they please, is surprising to a stranger, but pleasing withal, as they are usually handsome and healthy-looking. Turkeys will wander a long way from home, and return at night to roost as regularly as can be desired. Many farmers employ a boy to keep them from straying on the road or their neighbours' lands. Thus they obtain the greater part of their own living for about a month after harvest. When the fallen grain becomes scarcer, and the birds are unable to fill themselves, long troughs are provided at home, close to the roosting-place, which are filled with wheat and barley and a little maize. Thus they are ready for the birds when they return.

This treatment is continued until about the 1st of November, after which time they are fed as soon as liberated in the morning with a good feed of soft food, usually consisting of barley and wheat-meals. When satisfied they wander off to the fields until feeding-time in the afternoon, when they are provided with all the food they care to eat. About November 20th—that is, five weeks before Christmas—begins the final stage of the process. The turkeys are put up to fatten in a dry, comfortable shed, which must be large enough for the number of birds to be accommodated. Then the northern and eastern sides of this shed should be well closed in, but the southern and western sides may be wire netted, thus affording the inmates plenty of fresh air. Broad perches are provided, and must not be more than 3 feet above the ground. Food and water are placed in troughs conveniently situated, and away from the perches. When put up to fatten the turkeys are given all the food they will eat. The morning feed consists of barley-meal and wheat-meal. Some farmers who are very particular and have good customers mix the meals with milk, and give milk to drink instead of water, an inexpensive addition if skim milk is used, and one which considerably improves the flesh. Although not much used, there can be no doubt that the addition of a little pure fat to the soft food is highly beneficial, softening the flesh. Cooked potatoes can also be added to soft food with advantage, and this applies to all fowls put up for fattening. The afternoon feed consists of whole barley, oats, and a little maize, and these are more easily digested if steamed or soaked in hot water. When fully satisfied all food should be removed, and the troughs emptied, both morning and evening, and washed after the morning meal of soft food. In every case there must be a plentiful supply of coarse grit and sand available to the fowls, and a little slaked lime or old mortar will be an improvement. Without grit the turkeys cannot possibly digest their food properly, and without effective digestion flesh production will never be complete. Should any of the turkeys fight, the culprit or culprits must be removed. Turkeys can be crammed by machines as are fowls.

Madame Millet-Robinet, to whom reference has previously been made, thus describes the system of fattening turkeys in France. With all her recommendations we do not agree, but the information is of interest :—

"When the young birds become adults, that is to say are from six to seven months old, according to the season, which greatly influences their growth, one may fatten them advantageously. If one has a large flock of them, they should not all be put up to fatten at once, unless one wishes to send them all to market or nearly all together, which can only be done if in the neighbourhood of a large market where one is always able to sell whatever is sent. In all other cases, if one does not intend to send to market, but simply to fatten a few turkeys for private consumption, they should be marked on the foot by a piece of red thread tied round, in order to show those which are to be fattened.

"To indicate the different stages attained, it is necessary to add to the mark on the feet a few marks made with scissors on the feathers of the tail.

"The food to be given to turkeys is not the same during the whole time of fattening.

"During the first stage one must be content with giving them food on their return from the fields, for turkeys will not fatten in captivity, liberty is essential to them. They should be given waste grains of all kinds, potatoes and beetroots cut in small pieces, beech-nuts, small chestnuts; a fortnight later they should be given for their evening meal a paste of potatoes cooked and mashed and mixed with some meal. One may dilute this paste with curdled milk, but it is necessary to prepare only the quantity needed for each meal to prevent its turning sour.

"A fortnight after this change in the food, the grain in the morning, and on returning from the fields, should be left off, and replaced by the paste; at length during the last eight days, when the turkeys have eaten the paste, they should be made to swallow one or two pellets as an addition, and a pellet is added at every feed, so that at the end of a week the turkey eats, besides what it likes to take itself, 18 or 20 pellets, which are prepared as follows:—

"Dilute unsifted meal with curdled milk; this meal may be barley, wheat, buckwheat, or even maize. To this are added potatoes, steamed and mashed. This is formed into a paste, and after being kneaded well with the hands it is made up into patons or pellets about as big as a finger. These the turkey is made to swallow, taking care first to moisten them; for if one does not take this precaution they will not pass into the throat; then one gives it some milk.

"To cram several turkeys quickly two persons are necessary; one takes the bird between her knees, holding it in such a manner that it is facing her, and she opens its mouth carefully; the other takes the paton and places it into the throat, taking care not to raise the tongue of the bird and not to hurt it with her nails. It is necessary to make the patons pass into the stomach by pressing gently with the first finger and thumb along the neck of the turkey; and no part of the last paton must be left in the neck or crop of the bird; this can be told by pressing gently along the neck. As each fowl is crammed it is placed in a little run, so that there can be no mistake and no turkey can be crammed twice.

"*Mode of fattening in Provence.* In Provence and Flanders they give turkeys for fattening, besides ordinary food, nuts with their shells on. They commence by placing one in the beak, and press it with the thumb and first finger into the stomach. The next day they made them swallow two, then three, even to forty. They digest this food, but it gives their flesh a disagreeable and oily flavour. I do not hesitate to proscribe this practice.

" After the last week, that is to say after four or five weeks' fattening, turkeys should be perfectly fat."

The method of killing turkeys in Norfolk is, they are hung up by the legs, the wings being crossed to prevent struggling. Next they are given a sharp blow on the back of the head with a stout piece of wood, thus rendering them insensible. The knife is then inserted through the roof of the mouth, so as to pierce the brain. The majority are roughly plucked, all except the head, neck, and pinions. It is important to remember starving for several hours before the birds are killed.

GUINEA-FOWLS.

After the game season is over, in the early part of the year, there is a fair demand for guinea-fowls, or

Gallinas as they are often called, and at good prices, though their flesh is somewhat dry as compared with other poultry. They are a little difficult to deal with, and often pine if kept in confinement too closely. The best method of feeding up is to deal liberally with them during the winter, using oats and maize mixed, and then they will be in good condition. If a large, roomy shed is available they may be kept therein for a couple of weeks before killing, and fed upon oats. They are, as a rule, killed by paletting and the breasts should not be plucked.

CHAPTER XI.

MARKETING TABLE POULTRY.

It would be of no service producing any article of commerce unless we can place it where the natural return for our skill and labour is obtainable. Thus in every branch of industrialism, whether agricultural or manufacturing, the question of marketing is of great importance. I am inclined to the opinion that many of the troubles which affect rural pursuits are largely due to a lack of attention to this question. It has been pointed out previously that whilst in this country we have been content largely to run on lines which, however suitable to the conditions of a generation or two ago, are altogether unfitted to the circumstances of these times. And in this connection it must be borne in mind that foreign producers have learnt the necessity and value of proper organisation. Isolation is fatal to success in any industry where production is widely divided. Many instances could be cited in proof of this statement, but the fact is so obvious as to make it at once accepted. Wherever poultry keeping is a success, whether in relation to eggs or table poultry, some system has been adopted by which they are forwarded regularly and speedily to the point of distribution. Before the railway opened out the Heathfield district of Sussex carriers were employed, who landed the birds in London early on the morning after dispatch, and the quantity carried by them was enormous. Since the railway was available the work has been undertaken by it, and so great is the traffic that, as we have shown, the London, Brighton and South Coast Railway Company conveyed about 1,350 tons of dead fowls from the Heathfield station alone in twelve months. Without such arrangements it would have been impossible for the fattening industry to have increased as it has done, and the opportunity thus afforded has had a great influence in its development.

Of course the ideal would be in all industries that producers and consumers should come into direct and immediate contact, and in former days this was largely the case. But with the growth of great centres of population, and intercommunication between all parts of the country, this could only continue to a limited extent. Wherever possible, and this might be so to a greater extent than is generally supposed, direct sales should be made, to which end markets should be encouraged. But however much we may declaim against the middleman, he is a necessary factor, and so long as kept in his right position, that is, an intermediary between one class and another, and not a dominator, he serves a most useful purpose, earning well the commission allowed him and saving more than his cost. But if the result is at once to depreciate the return obtained by producers and enhance the cost to consumers unduly, then we have a serious state of things. In practice we know that better prices can be obtained from salesmen and dealers than others, more especially by those who have good produce to sell. Complaints are chiefly rife amongst those who send forward mediocre or poor qualities of any produce. We are bound, therefore, to recognise that it is to " the trade " we must look for help in this direction, and it is to the interest of that body to help forward a movement in the success of which they are so keenly interested.

Varied systems of marketing are to be met with in different parts of the country, and it is desirable to recognise this fact. Of course, where fattening establishments are in operation, and nearly all the fowls of the district pass through them, the owners understand what is needed, and prepare the fowls in accordance with market requirements. This gives them a decided advantage, as purchasers get what they want, and in the form which suits them best. We do not suggest that improvement should not be attempted ; that would be folly. But advance should be on lines that will propitiate rather than offend prejudice, and it is well to note that it is not so much what we like, but what our ultimate customers prefer and for which they are willing to pay. I am firmly convinced that whilst keeping the right breeds or crosses of poultry, and proper fattening of the fowls, are the first points to be kept in view, so that we may improve our home table poultry of all kinds, equally necessary is it that the birds shall be killed by the fattener, plucked, and sent to market dead. In every business economy of labour and trouble is most desirable ; and if we take the case of a retail poulterer, it would add greatly to his work if fowls were brought to him alive. When he can secure them killed, plucked, and shaped, they not only look better, but are better, and he has only the labour of dressing them in accordance with the needs of his customers. How desirable proper shaping is has already been shown in a previous chapter, and it is not too much to say that inattention on this point will go far towards destroying all that may be done in other directions.

It would be impossible to give descriptions of all the various ways in which poultry are marketed, but as representing different districts we have obtained the following particulars from provincial dealers. In the Metropolitan markets fowls must be sent dead and plucked to Smithfield or Leadenhall. The top prices are commanded by properly shaped Surrey fowls, and either this, or what is known as the Devonshire fashion, is essential. There is a good demand in London all the year round, but, of course, prices vary considerably.

Birmingham : (1) Chickens should be killed by breaking the neck, sent unplucked, packed in baskets with straw between each layer; (2) There is a good demand for young, well-fed poultry all the year round, the best prices being obtained in the spring ; (3) Fatted poultry not much in favour.

Cardiff: (1) The fowls should be simply killed, plucked, and roped ; (2) Most in demand during the autumn ; (3) Fatted fowls not in demand.

Cork: (1) Chickens not shaped, but are plucked, though some feathers are left on sides and tail; (2) January to June best season; (3) For general sale the birds are marketed as they come off the farm or run, not fatted.

Leeds: (1) The trade varies here. Birds must be killed by cutting the throat or bled in any other manner, and either simply plucked and clean picked, or shaped; (2) Chief demand from March onwards; (3) Fatted fowls are preferred if reasonable in price.

Leicester: (1) Chickens should be simply killed and plucked; (2) March to July best season; (3) Fatted fowls only in limited demand.

Manchester: (1) Young fowls are preferred, Surrey shaped for best trade, and command good prices; (2) March to August chief season, the high prices of "Surrey" chickens from November to February limiting demand; (3) Fatted fowls preferred.

Newcastle-on-Tyne: (1) Fowls are marketed killed, and roughly plucked; (2) Sell best when game is not in season; (3) Fatted fowls scarcely known.

Norwich: (1) On this market all fowls must be nicely plucked, but are not shaped; (2) A few early spring chickens are sold in April, May, and June, but most demand in the late autumn, after veal and lamb season is over, and all through the winter; (3) Although a great number of fowls are killed without any preparation, well-fatted fowls are certainly preferred.

We do not give the above in order to discourage attempts at improvement, but to show what is the state of things at the present time. The public taste can be educated, and though there might be some difficulty at first, the introduction of fatted and shaped fowls would ultimately exert an influence. Poultry producers should study their local markets, and wherever there are holiday resorts available, advantage should be taken to meet the special demand, which is generally a good one, though limited in respect to time. At such places there is nearly always a good market for summer ducks.

The time of year when poultry is marketed is an essential consideration. Again and again when complaints have been made as to the small prices received for chickens, has it been found that no thought had been given to the ruling rates at different periods of the year. Chickens are worth as a rule about twice as much in April as in August, and in this connection it is necessary to bear in mind that when the game comes in down go the prices for fowls. Ducklings should be marketed from January to June, and the difference between spring and summer prices for these succulent dainties is even greater than in the case of chickens. Geese and turkeys, of course, come into demand in the autumn, the top prices being realised about Christmas, and Guinea-fowls in February and March. To meet these requirements it is requisite to pay attention as to periods for breeding, but the successful man in every branch of life must study such questions in relation to marketing opportunities, and be prepared to live mentally months in advance.

As a rule fowls are plucked as soon as they are killed, and the feathers come out much more easily than would be the case later on. In Sussex nearly all the chickens are singed, the object being to get rid of the small hairs which cannot be plucked out. When properly done there can be no doubt that a fowl is considerably improved thereby, but care must be taken not to burn or blacken the flesh, or, in fact, to leave any signs of the operation. Good wheat straw is found to be the best for singeing.

The packing of poultry is where much harm may be done if not properly carried out. We have seen crates of chickens opened, and their value was materially reduced because of bad packing, many of the birds being "barked" or otherwise damaged. They ought to be packed firmly and evenly, and in this way will carry long distances in perfect safety. In this country strong willow baskets are usually employed, well lined out with straw, and with an abundance of straw beneath each row and on top. The birds are placed with the sterns to the sides, and in double rows. In France a firm crate, made of wood with straight rods fitted into a strong wooden frame, is employed, and these are at once light in weight and yet strong. They are well lined out with straight straw, but in nearly all cases each bird is wrapped in a fine linen cloth, and this does much to keep them from injury. We have seen cloths used here, and for the better class of fowls their use might with advantage be increased. During warm weather in France ice is largely used in packing, but that is seldom necessary in this country.

I should like to refer to a new industry which has recently sprung up at Bourg, in the La Bresse district of France. This is the tinning of fowls, and is due to M. Dupont, a large poultry dealer in that city. The tins are oval and made in different sizes, some containing a quarter of a fowl, sold at about 1s.; a half fowl, sold at about 2s.; and a whole fowl, sold at 4s., these being small-sized birds. Larger specimens are sold at 6 to 8 francs each. The birds are clean plucked, head and feet cut off, and dressed properly. They are then placed into a copper and boiled until nearly cooked, after which they are put into tins and covered with a very clear jelly, which is chiefly extracted from calves' feet. This hardens in about twenty-five minutes. The tins are next carefully soldered or sealed, and again cooked, this time in a copper or boiler, called an " autoclaire," in order to kill any germs. The fowls are ready for use on opening, and can be eaten either cold or heated. The flavour of these birds is excellent, and when taken out of the tin are embedded in their own jelly. I understand that in 1893, which was the first year that this industry was carried on, M. Dupont sold about 10,000 tins, whereas last year he sold about 30,000, sending them to all parts of Europe and America. There would seem to be an idea in this, and I commend it to those who are interested in the poultry question. Of course it may be assumed that M. Dupont tins the fowls at the time of year when they are lowest in price, and naturally does not put up the most expensive specimens in this way, but there can be no doubt as to the quality of the birds sent out.

Whilst it is true that the dressing and trussing of fowls is poulterers' work, and that whenever fowls are sold through the trade it is better left in their hands, as they can thus meet immediate demands, a work like this would be incomplete without some description of the methods adopted. Where chickens are sold direct to consumers it may be essential that they be trussed. Cooks as a rule, however, are equal to the work, or ought to be, for the preparation of fowls by poulterers in some cases has obviated the need for a cook knowing more than how to boil or roast. It is somewhat difficult to describe operations like these, but the following is an attempt in that direction.

For Roasting. Presuming that the chicken has been properly plucked, (1) nick the skin of each leg through to the bone, just below the joint ; (2) trim the pinions, cutting off the skin on outer side, so as to remove all marks of feather pits ; (3) lay chicken on its breast, with stern towards operator, and head away from the body ; (4) make a transverse cut in skin of neck about two inches from back, and lay skin thus loosened backwards, exposing vertebræ ; (5) cut off neck and head about two inches in front of previous cut, thus leaving about two inches of neck skin ; (6) now turn bird round sideways, breast upwards, and laying back the neck skin to expose the front of breast ; (7) press the thumb firmly down the Λ-shaped orifice thus exposed, loosen the skin, and insert finger into body to internal organs from breast-bone ; (8) carefully cut out merry-thought ; (9) turn bird round in the hand, make a transverse cut across the vent, immediately below the "parson's nose," and an angular cut at each side, which prevents the sides cracking when the bird is being drawn ; (10) insert forefinger and find "trail," which cut off, loosen the intestines gently but firmly, and draw through vent, taking care not to break any organ; (11) now place chicken on the table breast upwards, and insert long needle between thigh behind leg joint, pressing to corresponding place on other side, using fine string, and drawing through; (12) lay fowl over on table, and insert needle in first joint of wing, draw through and pass string over back, repeating on reverse side, here pull tight and tie up; (13) insert needle through body at end of back-bone, and at fore end of breast-bone, but in neither case is it necessary to pierce the meat on breast; (14) carry string round legs and tie, the legs standing away from behind the body; (15) chop off the toes; and (16) when the fowl is smoothed over by the hands it is complete.

For Boiling. With the exception that it is unnecessary to cut the legs, (1) proceed exactly as described for roasting to 10; (11) insert first and second fingers of one hand through vent, and loosen the skin on thigh up to hock on both legs. This is an easy operation, only needing a little care to prevent tearing the skin; (12) make a cut through skin on inside of each leg about an inch above hock knuckle, and right to bone; (13) also cut to bone of foot immediately above top toe; (14) take chicken in hand, turn lower leg, or shank, under thigh, feel with finger inserted under skin for cut in leg, and draw leg under skin, repeating this process on other side. The feet only will now protrude, and they should be cut off; (15) insert needle through front of body and stitch wings as in roast (11 and 12) chicken, but the wings may be shortened and inserted under skin as are the legs; (16) pass needle through thighs behind, and tie up on back in front of stern.

Boneing Fowls is a much more difficult process, and takes longer to perform, but when skilfully done leaves the meat unbroken or torn. The bird is treated as for roasting 1 to 5, but is not drawn, the organs remaining in carcass; (6) after cutting the neck, cut out the crop and merry-thought; (7) begin to strip the flesh off downward from neck, glove fashion, until wings are reached; (8) cut wing-bone through, just above second joint, and break it off; (9) turn bone backwards through the flesh, scrape it down as it proceeds, drawing it out completely, removing any splinters, repeating on other side; (10) resume stripping the flesh from carcass, holding upwards, until legs are reached; (11) these must in turn be turned inwards; (12) cut bone at joint, and scrape with knife, until bones can be removed; (13) continue stripping until scallop is reached, when it must be cut, and the carcass comes out complete; (14) the breast fillets must now be cut out carefully, and entirely off the keel or breast-bone; (15) take fowl by legs and turn right way out, placing fillets within; (16) roll up, and it is ready for use in whatever form desired.

In all these operations cleanliness of the board, and constant wiping, as required, of the parts are most desirable.

CHAPTER XII.

TABLE POULTRY EXHIBITIONS.

In another place * we have discussed the general question of poultry in connection with agricultural shows, and given various suggested classes, but our present purpose is to consider the subject entirely in its relation to table poultry.

Whenever possible, and this is certainly desirable at summer agricultural exhibitions, there ought to be classes for live poultry as well as for dead, whilst at the winter fat stock shows the better plan may be to confine the exhibition to dressed poultry. In connection with the classes for live fowls, we believe that it is much better to confine them to pure breeds, as the basis for first-class table fowls should be pure races. As a matter of education, however, it may be worth while to give classes for first crosses, in order to show what these are like. The following classes are suggested as providing for both live and dead poultry at,

* "Poultry Keeping as an Industry for Farmers and Cottagers" (Edward Arnold), chap. xix.

say, a summer show, and will be found to cover the ground pretty completely.

No. 1. Complete List.

Live Poultry.
Dorkings, dark or coloured.
 „ silver-grey.
Old-fashioned Game.
Indian Game.
French.
Any other Pure Breed.
Aylesbury Ducks.
Rouen Ducks.
Geese.
Turkeys.

Dressed Poultry.
Dorkings.
Game or Indian Game.
French.
Crosses with Dorkings.
Crosses with Game or Indian Game.
Crosses with French.
Ducks.
Geese.
Turkeys.

No. 2 List.

Live Poultry.
Dorkings.
Old-fashioned Game.
Indian Game.
French.
Any other Pure Breed.
Ducks.
Geese.
Turkeys.

Dressed Poultry.
Dorkings.
Game or Indian Game.
Any other Pure Breed.
Any Cross-bred Fowl.
Ducks.
Geese or Turkeys.

This latter might be modified still further, but we think that any show adopting this system would be able to arrange for the number of classes here indicated. In all cases the dead poultry should be shown in couples, and it is better to have separate classes for cockerels and pullets.

Of course much may be done in extending the number of classes given. The finest show which has ever been held in this country up to the present time, was in connection with the Smithfield Christmas Fat Cattle Show, held in December, 1894. This was under the patronage of H.R.H. the Prince of Wales, and was managed by a committee of which Sir Walter Gilbey, Bart., was Chairman. In this case no live fowls at all were exhibited, and the following classification may be drawn as indicating a complete covering of the ground. The show was a very great success, both as to the number of entries and the interest manifested.

Class.
1. Dorking. Couple of Cockerels.
2.   ,,   Couple of Pullets.
3. Old English Game. Couple of Cockerels.
4.   ,,   Couple of Pullets.
5. Indian Game. Couple of Cockerels.
6.   ,,   Couple of Pullets.
7. Any Pure Breed other than above. Couple of Cockerels.
8.   ,,   ,,   ,,   Couple of Pullets.
9. Old English Game and Dorking. Couple of Cockerels.
10.   ,,   ,,   ,,   Couple of Pullets.
11. Indian Game and Dorking. Couple of Cockerels.
12.   ,,   ,,   Couple of Pullets.
13. Surrey or Sussex Fowls. Couple of Cockerels.
14.   ,,   ,,   Couple of Pullets.

15. Any other Cross-bred than those mentioned in Classes 9 to 14. The Breeding to be stated, if known. Couple of Cockerels.
16. Any Cross-bred other than those mentioned in Classes 9 to 14. The Breeding to be stated, if known. Couple of Pullets.
17. Irish Fowls. Any variety bred and fed in Ireland. Couple of Cockerels.
18. Irish Fowls. Any variety bred and fed in Ireland. Couple of Pullets.
19. Capons. Any variety, Breed to be stated, if known. Couple.
20. Aylesbury Ducks. Couple of Drakes or Ducks.
21. Rouen Ducks. Couple of Drakes or Ducks.
22. Any Pure-bred variety other than Aylesbury or Rouen, the Breed to be stated. Couple of Drakes or Ducks.
23. Any Cross-bred variety. The Breeding to be stated, if known. Couple of Drakes or Ducks.
24. Toulouse Geese. Couple of Ganders or Geese.
25. Embden Geese. Couple of Ganders or Geese.
26. Any Cross-bred variety. The Breeding to be stated, if known. Couple of Ganders or Geese.
27. Turkeys Cocks, Bronze. Couple.
28. Turkeys Hens, Bronze. Couple.
29. Turkeys Cocks, other than Bronze. Couple.
30. Turkeys Hens, other than Bronze. Couple.
31. Guinea-fowls. The breast only to be plucked. Couple.
32. English Pigeons. Two Couple.
33. English Tame Rabbits. To be paunched, not skinned. Couple.
34. Turkeys. Six Birds of one Breed or Cross.
35. Geese. Six Birds of one Breed or Cross.
36. Pure-bred Fowls. Six Birds of one Breed.
37. Cross-bred Fowls. Six Birds of the same Cross.
38. Ducks. Six Birds of one Breed or Cross.

So far as the rules and regulations are concerned, one or two points should be referred to, namely, that the birds were to have been bred in the year 1894; that they must have been in the possession of the exhibitor one month before the day of the show; the specimens were to be sent killed and plucked, except upon the head and neck, and might be shaped for market, but not drawn or scalded, the breast-bones were not to be broken, nor the head, comb, or feet cut off or scalded; the judges were instructed to regard quality of flesh and smallness of bone and offal as of primary importance. It was provided that not more than one entry could be made in the same class by the same exhibitor, but we think that some modification might be made of this rule where more than one breed is exhibited in a class.

A very important development in connection with a show of this kind, as seen at the Smithfield Exhibition, was the prices for which the birds were sold by auction, and there was a considerable amount of interest manifested in this, large numbers being purchased at high prices, higher than anything previously known in this country.

Wherever dead poultry are exhibited, the utmost care should be taken to keep everything about the place as sweet and clean as possible, as it is desirable to lay them out in such a manner as they will be best displayed. Benches are better when built in two tiers with a slight slope, so as to show the birds lying thereon. These benches or tables should be covered with linen cloths, and there ought to be cloths so that the exhibits may be covered, if the show is prolonged more than one day. We do not approve of the plan of taking the winning birds away from the others, because everything should be measured by comparison, and it is desirable by those little things which need scarcely be mentioned to make the show as attractive as possible. An increased interest can be obtained if demonstrations are given during the show in shaping and dressing poultry.

In respect to the judging of table poultry, there are one or two points which require to be considered. At the outset it would seem that the best persons to judge table poultry would necessarily be poulterers, but though there are exceptions to this rule, we think that on the whole poulterers are not the most suitable judges. For one thing, few of them have any actual knowledge as to the different breeds of poultry, which knowledge is an essential when birds of different varieties are on exhibition. The poulterer who may be able to pick out a first-class table fowl, if he were unable to determine whether it was of the breed as provided by the schedule, would not be properly qualified for his duties. We think, therefore, that this matter must be taken into consideration, and whilst the most perfect judge would be a poulterer who has given study to poultry as live stock as well as dead, failing him we should prefer a poultry breeder who knows something about table fowls. Quality ought always to be preferred to mere size.

INDEX.

	PAGE		PAGE
ACCOMMODATION for ducklings	111	Collecting cage (Sussex)	64
American duck farm	118	Colour of skin and flesh	30
Aylesbury duck industry	108	Concentration in industries	19
		Contracts for ducks eggs	111
BAILEY, Mr. J., on *petits poussins*	104	County Council lectures	72
Black Norfolk turkey	129	Cramming geese	127
Boneing chickens	146	,, turkeys	133
Bone, light, desirable	32	,, by funnel	80
Breeds and crosses	29	,, by machine	66, 67, 83
Broilers	105	,, by *patons*	80
Bronze American turkey	129	,, in Sussex	66
Brooders	48	Crosses	39
Broody hens	43		
Brooke Bros., sales by	19	DEMONSTRATIONS at shows	152
Brooke's, Mr. C. E., fattening shed	55	Devereux, Mr. T., on *petits poussins*	101
Buckwheat meal	83	Dorkings	33
		Dressing poultry	143
CAGES for fattening	50, 52	Ducks	108
Calway's pen	54	Duckers	109
Cambridge bronze turkey	129	Duck farm in Lancashire	115
Capons and poulardes	76, 77		
Celery-fed ducks	119	EAST Anglia, geese in	121
Chicken house	47	Embden geese	120
Chicken rearing	47	England, poultry fattening in	63
Classification at shows	148		

	PAGE
Exhibitions of table poultry	147
FARMS, size of, in France	73
Fasting before killing	71, 87
Fat for fattening	65, 71
"Fatted Fowl" in Scripture	13
Fattening districts	16, 50
" establishments, influence of	23
" geese	122, 125
" house at Baynards	55
" turkeys	130
" by ancient Egyptians	13
" and killing house at Gambais	59
Faverolles	100
Feeding broilers	105
Flesh-forming qualities	32
Food for ducklings	112
" used in fattening	65, 71
"Forester" incubator	46
France, fattening fowls in	73
French shaping	91, 94
Funnel for cramming	80
GAMBAIS poultry school	59
Game fowls	36
Geese	120
German fattening establishment	59
Ground oats	64, 117
Guinea-fowls	134
HATCHING and rearing	41

	PAGE
Hatching ducklings	111
"Hearson" crammer	67
" incubator	45
Higglers	41
INCREASE in weight by cramming	68
Incubators	43
Indian Game	35
Interior, Heathfield shed	55
Irish chickens in Sussex	23, 72
JUDGING table poultry	152
"KEAY'S" incubator	46
Killing	85
" geese	123
" turkeys	134
LA BRESSE	38
" dead poultry	96
La Flèche	37
" dead poultry	93
Lancashire duck farm	115
Lean fowls should not be killed	14
Leighton Buzzard duck industry	108
Local supplies	17
London the great market	17, 26
MARKETING	27, 136
Markham, Gervasse, on geese	120
Marten's shed	53
Middlemen	137

INDEX.

	PAGE
Milk for fattening	65, 71
"Monarch" incubator	45
NETTLES, use of	66, 71
Neve crammer	66
OATS, ground	64
Objections to fattening	27
Odile-Martin fattening cage	83
Open-air cages	52
PACKING poultry	142
Paletting	87
Patons, cramming by	80
Petits poussins	98
Plan of Baynards pens	57
Plucking	95
,, geese	123
Potatoes	80
Poulardes	76, 77
Poultrykeepers and fattening establishments	23
,, markets in France	75
,, rearing ,,	42
Preface	5
"Premier" incubator	45
Prices for ducklings,	110, 114
,, for fatted fowls	15
,, of geese	122
,, of Sussex fowls,	20, 21
,, of turkeys	128, 130
Profitable nature of industry	25
Provincial markets	139
RAILWAY traffic from Heathfield and Uckfield	22, 23

	PAGE
Rawson, Mr. J. S., on killing geese	123
Rearing chickens	47
Rew's, Mr. R. H., report,	18, 21
Rules for fattening	70
SALES by Messrs. Brooke Bros.	19, 20
Selling young chickens	49
Shaping	88
,, geese	124
Sheds and pens	50
Singeing	97
Size of turkeys	128
Skim milk, value of	66
"Soft bill" in ducklings	113
Spencer's, Mr. Aubrey, report	109
Sussex fowls	35
,, ,, average values of	20, 21
Sussex poultry	18
Structure of fowl	29, 31
Supplies of poultry in Britain	16
TABLE poultry exhibitions	147
,, ,, trade in France	78
Tallow greaves for duck feeding	113, 117
Technical education	28, 74
Time of year to market	141
Tinning fowls	143
Toulouse geese	121
Trade in Sussex poultry	22
Trough for shaping	88
Trussing fowls	143
,, for boiling	145

	PAGE		PAGE
Trussing, for roasting	144	"Westmeria" incubator	46
Turkeys	128	Whey for fattening	79
		White turkey	129
WEIGHTS of fatted poultry	39	Winter eggs	44

J. W. COOK,
THE WORLD-FAMED HIGH-CLASS POULTRY BREEDER,
LINCOLN, ENGLAND,

HAS over 1,000 PRIZE-BRED PULLETS and COCKERELS FOR SALE, at moderate prices. All varieties reared on the 400 Acre Farm. FOWLS FOR FATTENING supplied. EGGS FOR SITTING in season. *Catalogue free.*—Address. J. W. COOK, B. P., Lincoln, England.

The "Forester" Incubator,

FOR HATCHING ANY DESCRIPTION OF POULTRY, GAME, AND OTHER EGGS.

Heat automatically regulated; eggs turned mechanically, all in three seconds; thermometer adjustable in position for eggs of any size; hatching seen through glass lid; no hot-water tank nor lamp glass; small consumption of oil; high percentage of hatching; hardy and vigorous broods. Size for 48 eggs, price **£2s. 6d.**

The "Forester" Foster=Mother

covers 20 square feet, and may be enlarged at pleasure; only about 2ft. × 2ft. × 2ft. when packed; ready for use in five minutes; easily moved; no water tank; lamp guaranteed to keep alight in the roughest wind. Price **50s.**

Catalogue of Appliances, with high testimonials, 1d. stamp; *Descriptive Pamphlet*, 6d. stamps.

J. F. A. ROBERTS & CO.,
Lyndhurst, New Forest.

ESTABLISHED OVER FORTY YEARS.

JAS. CHAMBERLIN & SMITH

Pheasant and Poultry Food Merchants,

POST OFFICE STREET, NORWICH.

Sole Proprietors of the Celebrated Aromatic Spanish Meal, D. S. Meat Greaves, Kalyde, Canadian Poultry Meal, Caycar Excelsior, &c.

Received the Only Award for Game and Poultry Foods from International Jury, Paris Exhibitions, 1878 and 1889.
Bronze Medal and Diploma, Mannheim, 1880.   Silver Medal, Cleves, 1881.
Gold Medal and Diploma of the Société Belge Avicultura, 1884.
Silver Medal, Antwerp Exhibition, 1885.

CANADIAN POULTRY MEAL.

The Cheapest and Best Food in the World for POULTRY of EVERY KIND.

CHAMBERLIN & SMITH'S ROUP PILLS.

For Poultry, Pigeons and Cage Birds.—Roup is known to be one of the great scourges of the poultry yard, but these Pills will be found a certain cure in the majority of cases for Roup, Cold in the Head, Bronchitis, and other respiratory affections. They are carefully prepared from a reliable recipe, and will be found the best cure for Roup.

One Shilling per Bottle; Post Free, 1s. 2d.

CHAMBERLIN & SMITH'S CONDITION PILLS.

For Poultry, Pigeons, and Cage Birds.—These Pills are invaluable, and should be given in all cases of debility, digestive derangements, skin affections, and as a general tonic; also for getting birds into condition for exhibition. A dose of these Pills given before and after a journey, or during the prevalence of very severe weather, will often prevent serious disease.

One Shilling per Bottle; Post Free, 1s. 2d.

These Medicines are packed in specially prepared bottles, which are sent out in wooden cases. *Can be obtained of all Chemists, Corn Dealers, &c.*

HAVE IT ALWAYS BY YOU.   AN INFALLIBLE CURE FOR GAPES.

KALYDE

Is prepared from the recipe of one of the most experienced Gamekeepers in England, and never known to fail to CURE the GAPES.

KALYDE is an extremely volatile powder, the product of valuable mineral and Indian vegetable substance.

It should be used upon the first appearance of Gape symptoms. It is very easily administered.

Sold in Tins, weighing about 2 lbs., 2s. each. Post free, 2s. 6d.

Dear Sirs,—I have tried your Gape Cure, Kalyde, and found it gives great satisfaction. I tried it on a coop of young chickens that had it very bad, almost skeletons, and it quite cured them. I can recommend it very highly. I think it will be a great success.—CHARLES HUNT, Gamekeeper to Lord Hastings.

KALYDE is only prepared by JAS. CHAMBERLIN & SMITH,

Game, Poultry & Dog Food Manufacturers, Post Office St., Norwich.

BOULTON & PAUL, NORWICH.
THE ORIGINAL MAKERS OF KENNEL AND POULTRY APPLIANCES.

Our Original Portable Fowls' House.

Reduced Cash Prices of House only, Carriage Paid.

No. 14.	4 ft. square	…	…	…	…	£2 15 0
No. 15.	5 ft.	„	…	…	…	3 10 0
No. 16.	6 ft.	„	…	…	…	4 15 0

If mounted on Wheels, 10s. extra.

NOTICE.—The price of this House has been considerably reduced to come within the means of all Poultry Keepers. We shall continue to supply this House constructed as hitherto, and of best materials and workmanship. It cannot be compared with the cheaply constructed Houses that are advertised in the papers at ridiculously low prices.

Cash Prices of Runs only, Carriage Paid.

Run 22 ft. by 18 ft. for No. 14 Houses, with Hurdles, Gate, Angle
    Pillars and Trough … … … … … … £3 9 6
Run 20 ft. by 19 ft. for No. 15 Houses, ditto ditto … … 4 0 0
Run 30 ft. „ 20 ft. „ No. 16 „ ditto ditto … … 4 10 6

If with Galvanized Sheet Iron at bottom as shown, 1s. per yard extra.

No. 45a. Fattening Pen.

Fitted with movable drawer, so arranged that the Pens can always be kept sweet and clean. The troughs are galvanized and loose for cleaning purposes.

Cash Price. ... 30/-
For Four Fowls.
Two Pens Carriage Paid.

Cheap Game Proof & Chicken Hurdles. No. 180.

1 in. Mesh.
Cash Prices.
6 ft. long, 2 ft. 6 in. high, ea. 2 6
6 ft. long, 3 ft. high … „ 3 -

All Orders amounting to 40s. value Carriage Paid to the principal Railway Stations in England and Wales.

SEND FOR ILLUSTRATED CATALOGUE FREE ON APPLICATION.

Boulton & Paul, Norwich.

BARNARD BISHOP & BARNARDS, Ld.,

MANUFACTURERS OF EVERY REQUISITE FOR

Poultry, Pigeons, Rabbits, and Dogs on the most approved principles.

FULLY ILLUSTRATED CATALOGUE FREE ON APPLICATION.

NEW POULTRY HOUSE with COVERED RUN, No. 92.

A most complete and artistic house.
5 ft. 6 wide, 10 ft. long £4 5 0
6 ft. 6 „ 12 ft. 6 „ 5 15 0
Carriage paid.

Corrugated iron 2 ft. high round front and sides of run, 6s. and 8s. 6d. extra respectively.

NEW PORTABLE FOWLS' HOUSE AND RUN, No. 107.

Awarded Silver Medal, Dairy Show, 1894.

House 4 ft. 6 by 3 ft. 6, Run, 9 ft. long. House fitted with splined floor, outside nest boxes, &c., complete as shown, £3 carriage paid.

IMPROVED FATTENING COOP, No. 138.

Birds fatten naturally and quickly in these coops, and put on flesh instead of fat only as when cramming is resorted to.

For 4 Birds, 30s.; for 6 Birds, 37s. 6d. carriage paid.

The Favourite CHICKEN NURSERY, COCKEREL PEN, RABBIT or CAVY HUTCH, No. 128.

6 ft. long, 3 ft. wide, 25s. each. Two sent carriage paid.

NORFOLK IRON WORKS, NORWICH; and 91 and 95, Queen Victoria St., LONDON, E.C.

Four Gold Medals.   Silver and Bronze Medals.

THE WESTMERIA INCUBATOR
For 56, 108, and 216 EGGS.

Hatched at the Royal Show 89 per Cent.; and at the Dairy Show 93 per Cent.

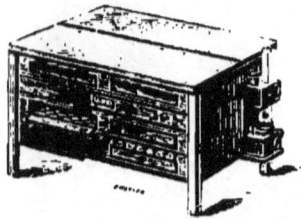

"It hatched all the ducks' Eggs put in."—SIR FREDERICK MUSGRAVE, Eden Hall, Cumberland.

"I am more than satisfied."—HENRY DIGBY, ESQ., Huddersfield.

"I am delighted with it."—E. F. ELLIOTT, ESQ., Pleydon, near Rye.

THE WESTMERIA BROODER.

"No one having tried it will use any other." The DUCHESS OF WELLINGTON.

"The most perfect I know."—LADY PHILLIMORE, Botley.

"By far the best. No exhibitor should be without one."—G. H. PROCTER, ESQ. Durham.

CRAMMING MACHINE.

For the Artificial Fattening of Fowls and Turkeys. (Nere's Patent.)

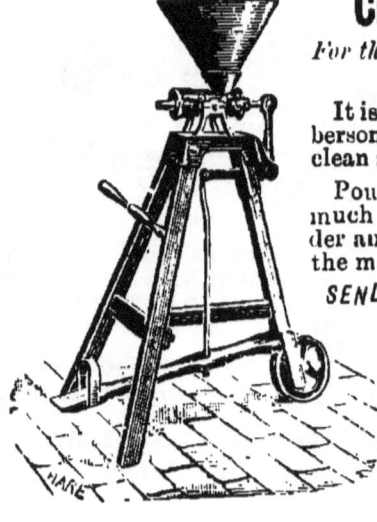

It is strongly made, without being cumbersome; simple in design, it is easily kept clean; and can be worked by one man.

Poultry thus fed is ready for the table much sooner; and being beautifully tender and fleshy will fetch the top price in the market.

SEND PENNY STAMP FOR COMPLETE LIST.

WESTMERIA Co.,
Leighton Buzzard,
ENGLAND.

TELEGRAPHIC ADDRESS—
"Nourishment, London."

TELEPHONE 11784.

BANKERS:
The City Bank,
Threadneedle St.,
LONDON.

CHARLES E. BROOKE & SONS,

POULTRY SALESMEN,

GAME AND MEAT FACTORS,

ALSO DEALERS IN

Quails, Pigeons, Rabbits, Venison, &c.,

39, LEADENHALL MARKET, LONDON.

Every information given concerning market prices and prospects and prompt attention paid to country orders.

ENGLISH AND FOREIGN CORRESPONDENCE INVITED.

IMPORTANT
To Poultry Keepers and Game Raisers.

BROWN'S AROMATIC COMPOUND for Poultry, Game, &c., is found of immense benefit to all keepers of birds who use it; the best article ever sold to secure eggs throughout the winter, assist the process of **Moulting**, and should be given to all fowls put up for **Fattening**. Has stood the test of a quarter of a century. Testimonials from a large number of leading breeders. A 10s. tin sufficient for 1300 birds for a week; 1s. tin per week for 100 fowls. Sold in tins—No. 1, 1s. 3d.; No. 2, 2s. 9d.; No. 3, 5s. 6d.; No. 4, 10s.; No. 5, 20s., all carriage paid. The larger sizes much cheaper than the others.

AROMATIC TONIC PASTE and ROUP PILLS for Poultry and Game when out of sorts. Nothing better on the market. Boxes 6d. and 1s.; post free 8d. and 1s. 3d.

CAPSULES OF GUARANTEED QUALITY, the purest and most effective remedies known for Dogs, Poultry, Pigeons, and Cage Birds. Sorts—Cod Liver Oil, Cod Liver Oil with Quinine, Castor Oil, Charcoal, Astringent, Copaiba, Turpentine, Areca Nut, Oil of Male Fern, Santonin. Made in 4 sizes. Lists on application. 1s. per box, post free 1s. 1½d. Six boxes, 5s.

E. T. BROWN & SON, 31, Dean St., Newcastle-on-Tyne, England.

Wholesale Agents—London: BARCLAY & SONS, LTD., FARRINGDON STREET, E.C.; SANGER & SONDEN, OXFORD STREET, W.

HEARSON'S PATENT CHAMPION INCUBATOR

FOR HATCHING POULTRY, GAME, OR OSTRICHES.

Prices:			£	s.	d.
No. 1, to hold 13 Eggs	....		2	15	0
,, 2, ,, 25 ,,	....		4	7	6
,, 6, ,, 50 ,,	....		7	10	0
,, 11, ,, 100 ,,	....		10	3	0
,, 20, ,, 200 ,,	....		10	10	0

HEARSON'S Patent CHAMPION FOSTER MOTHER.
Price £5 5s.

HEARSON'S PATENT Cramming Machine.

For the Forced Feeding of Fowls, Turkeys, &c.

Price £4 10s.

HEARSON'S PATENT ROTARY PEN
for 30 Birds.

In our Rotary Pen each bird has a separate compartment, from which he never moves from the time he is put up to fatten until he is considered in condition for the table. The pen revolves on a vertical axis. Provision is made for collecting the droppings, so that there need be no offensive smell.

Price £10 10s.

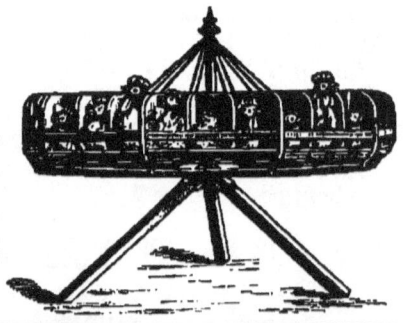

Poultry Breeders and others interested in the subject of Artificial Incubation should send for a copy of *THE PROBLEM SOLVED*. This work, beautifully illustrated, gives a minute description of all these apparatus, with full instructions for hatching and rearing poultry. Price, per post, 1s. 3d.

ADDRESS—D Department, CHAS. HEARSON & CO., Limited, 235, Regent Street, London, W.

BY
HER MAJESTY'S

ROYAL LETTERS
PATENT.

Pocock's Patent Egg Boxes.

With Interior Fittings of Felt.

FOR ROAD, RAIL, OR POST.

Two First Prizes London Dairy Shows.

MADE TO CARRY FROM 1 TO 80 DOZENS.

For Parcels Post to carry One Sitting of 13, Price 1/-; post free, 1/4½.

For Parcels Post, to carry Two Sittings, 26 Eggs, Price 1/10; Post free, 2/4.

Our "Hammock" Box, for Parcels Post.

To Carry One Dozen, price 10d.; post free, 1s. 2½d.

They may be
DROPPED ABOUT,
KICKED ABOUT,
KNOCKED ABOUT,
Without Damage to a Single Egg.

DAIRY OUTFIT CO., LIMITED,
KING'S CROSS, LONDON, N.

(Late FREETH & POCOCK, of VAUXHALL, LONDON.)

www.ingramcontent.com/pod-product-compliance
Lightning Source LLC
Chambersburg PA
CBHW030258170426
43202CB00009B/788